Fighter Pilots of World War I

Robert Jackson

Fighter Pilots of World War I

ST. MARTIN'S PRESS
New York

Copyright © 1977 by Robert Jackson
All rights reserved. For information, write:
St. Martin's Press, Inc., 175 Fifth Ave., New York, N.Y. 10010
Printed in Great Britain
Library of Congress Catalog Card Number: 77–76641
First published in the United States of America in 1977

Library of Congress Cataloging in Publication Data

Jackson, Robert, 1941–
    Fighter pilots of World War I.

   1. European War, 1914–1918—Aerial operations.
2. Air pilots—Biography. I. Title.
D600.J33   940.4′4′0922 [B]   77–76641
ISBN 0–312–28874–3

Contents

Introduction

It was a young man's war. A war of split-second judgement and skill, where boys barely out of school locked in deadly combat high over the shell-scarred earth of Flanders – and quickly learned that their new element, the sky, was terribly unforgiving of any mistake or foolhardiness. When they fell, they fell like meteors, their passage marked by a banner of smoke and white-hot flames from which the only escape was to jump to a less agonizing death, for in those days there were no parachutes.

As time passed, those who survived became old men in their twenties; veterans who knew all the tricks of their trade, who knew that the passport to survival was caution and who chopped their less experienced enemies from the sky with deadly efficiency. Some flew full at the throat of death, roving far across the enemy lines in search of their prey until their cinders, too, were scattered over the war-torn ground. A few – a very few – lived to pass on the lessons they had learned to future generations of combat pilots.

This is the story of some of those young men – British, French, American and German – who fought for mastery of the sky between 1914 and 1918: the Aces whose names are legendary even today.

1 Max Immelmann: Eagle of Lille

Ensign Max Immelmann had one big fear: that the war would be over before he could get into it. It was six weeks since the victorious German armies had advanced into Belgium, and it seemed to the impatient Immelmann that he was doomed to spend the rest of his military service on garrison duties while others did all the fighting. On 27 September 1914 he wrote to his mother:

> 'I am leading the thoroughly dull life of a hermit, and into the bargain I am in the stupidest thing God ever created – railway service! An enquiry went round as to whether anyone wanted to volunteer for infantry service, and I applied. It is by no means certain that I shall get a transfer to the infantry, but I should certainly like one, for it is really no joke to do nothing but play the railwaymen's overseer here.'

So, with an air of weary disillusionment, began the military career of a young man who, within six months, would rise to fame like a meteor – not in the mud and blood of no-man's land, but in the sky over Flanders. A man whose prowess would write one of the first chapters in the textbook of air combat, and earn him an immortal title – Immelmann: Eagle of Lille.

As a personality, Immelmann was fairly untypical of

the German youth of his day. Born in Dresden in September 1890, the eldest of three children, he soon displayed a passion for anything mechanical; he would sit for hours as a child meticulously taking clocks and toys apart and putting them back together again. He never left a job half-finished, a trait of thoroughness and perseverance he inherited from his father, who died when Max was seven.

From his mother he inherited, above all, a deep sense of duty. She was a remarkable woman, and something of a nonconformist. During the hard years of bringing up her children alone, she taught them to find out things for themselves; she believed that the world was changing, that the young had to change with it, and that the old values would soon be swept aside. She believed in fitness, too, feeding the children on a simple vegetarian diet and hardening them by physical exercise. This had the desired effect on Max, who radiated health and strength despite his small stature.

His love of mechanics persisted through his schooldays, when he achieved consistently high marks in the sciences and low marks in everything else. In 1905 he entered the Dresden Cadet School, where self-reliance and power of leadership were added to his qualities. On graduating in April 1911 he joined the Second Railway Regiment at Schöneberg, near Berlin – a choice of unit dictated by his urgent desire for practical technical work.

His service in the Railway Regiment, however, was destined to be a disappointment right from the start. Apart from the fact that a great deal of time was spent on drill and lectures on military tactics, engineering work had to be done in accordance with certain well-defined rules and procedures which left no scope for initiative or innovation. The one highlight came when, during a term with the War Academy in 1912, his class visited an airfield.

'One seldom sees anything so splendid,' he wrote. 'They showed us all the most important machines, such as the Wrights, Rumplers and Farmans, explained their construction and demonstrated three of them. It was a glorious and unique sight when these aeroplanes, which resembled huge birds, soared into the air and executed daring turns and glides with a truly amazing self-confidence.'

It all contributed to Max's disenchantment with army life, and in April 1912 he resigned from his regiment and began studying at Dresden's Technical High School. The next two and a half years were probably the happiest in Max's life. Not only was he able to indulge his passion for engines to the full; he was also able to devote much time to the Technical Aviation Association, experimenting with flying models and helping to organize the aviation meetings which were fast becoming popular in Germany.

Then came August 1914, and the outbreak of war. Both Max and his younger brother, Franz, immediately applied to join the Aviation Corps – but a fortnight later Max was called up to his old unit, the 2nd Railway Regiment, and there he languished until the beginning of November, when he received his long-awaited posting to the Aviation Recruit Centre at Adlershof. After going through the selection procedure he went on to the Military Aviation School at Johannistal to begin his flying training.

Despite his technical ability, Immelmann soon proved himself far from proficient as a student pilot. He was never consistent, and seemed unable to make himself at home in his new environment. Each of his landings was an event that the whole airfield turned out to watch, laying odds on whether or not Immelmann would break his aircraft. Nevertheless, Max enjoyed his flying and he was fortunate in having instructors who realized that prowess would

3

come in time. On 31 January 1915 he was finally allowed to go solo after making fifty-four dual flights – far in excess of the normal number.

In February he went back to Adlershof for an advanced flying course. He made another forty-five flights, but was still far from competent – as was quickly shown when an officer came to select advanced students for operational service at the front. Every candidate was required to make a demonstration flight, and Immelmann's went well until the landing, when his undercarriage got catastrophically tangled up with a manure heap. The aircraft went over on its back and was a total loss, although the pilot escaped with only his pride injured. 'Now I can sit at home for several weeks more for certain,' he wrote ruefully. 'But that's the way of it: I have 130 smooth landings to my credit, and for the 131st, on which everything depends, I make a crash....'

It was the middle of March 1915 before he was finally transferred to an operational airfield. His new base was Rethel, in France's beautiful Aisne Valley, and apart from the rumble of distant bombardments in the direction of Rheims it was all very peaceful. Immelmann, flying an LVG two-seater, had the principal task of ferrying mail and spare parts to other units, and it was during one of these flights – on 25 March – that he had his first sight of the enemy: a French Farman biplane, some hundreds of feet higher up. Max was deterred from investigating further by the intense German anti-aircraft fire, which came closer to hitting him than the Frenchman.

In May 1915, after an uneventful spell of duty as an artillery spotter pilot, Immelmann was sent to Döberitz to join a new Air Corps unit, *Fliegerabteilung* (Flying Section) 62. The Section, which was equipped with LVG biplanes, included some of Germany's most promising young pilots; among them was Lieutenant Oswald

Boelcke, with whom Immelmann was to become firm friends.

At this time a major Allied offensive was under way in the Arras sector, and as soon as it was considered operational Section 62 was ordered to an airfield near Douai to fly in support of the hard-pressed German forces. In the spring of 1915 the Allies enjoyed a considerable measure of air superiority over the battlefield, thanks mainly to new air fighting tactics pioneered by the French, who operated in flights of three or four aircraft under the control of a designated leader. The Germans, on the other hand, tended to operate singly, which made them relatively easy prey. Immelmann himself had a narrow escape on 2 June, when his aircraft was attacked over the front line by a French Farman biplane. He managed to get away, although his LVG was riddled with bullets.

The German inferiority in the air was not to last. In July 1915 a new aircraft appeared at the front: the Fokker E2 monoplane, the first German machine specifically designed for air fighting. Owing to a newly-devised synchronization gear, it had a machine-gun that fired directly through the arc of the propeller – which meant that the Fokker pilot could use his whole aircraft as an aiming platform.

Immelmann's chance to test the Fokker in action came on 1 August, when he took off with Boelcke to attack some British aircraft which were bombing the German airfield at Douai. The subsequent combat report tells the story:

'At 6 am on 1 August Lieutenant Immelmann took off in a Fokker fighting monoplane in order to drive away the numerous (about ten to twelve) enemy machines which were bombing Douai aerodrome. He succeeded in engaging three machines showing French markings in the area between Arras and Vitry. Heedless

5

of the odds against him, he made an energetic and dashing attack on one of them at close quarters. Although this opponent strove to evade his onslaught by glides and turns and the other two enemy aircraft tried to assist the attacked airman by machine-gun fire, Lieutenant Immelmann finally forced him to land westward of and close to Brebières after scoring several hits on vital parts of the machine. The inmate, an Englishman (instead of an observer he had taken with him a number of bombs, which he had already dropped), was severely wounded by two cross-shots in his left arm. Lieutenant Immelmann immediately landed in the neighbourhood of the Englishman, took him prisoner and arranged for his transport to the Field Hospital of the 1st Bavarian Reserve Corps. The machine was taken over by the section. There was no machine-gun on board. A sighting device for bomb-dropping has been removed and will be tested.'

This victory of Immelmann's was significant in that it was the first scored by a pilot flying an aircraft specifically designated as a fighter or 'scout' machine. Although there were several more skirmishes during the weeks that followed, it was the end of August before he gained his second victory. He described what happened in a letter to his mother:

'...Suddenly I saw an enemy biplane attack Boelcke from behind. Boelcke did not seem to have seen him. As if by agreement, we both turned round. First he came into Boelcke's sights, then into mine, and finally we both went for him and closed up on him to within fifty to eighty metres. Boelcke's gun appeared to have jammed, but I fired 300 rounds. Then I could hardly believe my eyes when I saw the enemy airman throw up both his arms. His crash helmet fell out and went down in wide circles, and a second later the machine plunged headlong into the depths from 2,200 metres. A pillar of dust showed where he hit the ground....'

By the end of October 1915 Immelmann had increased his score to five, and the German propaganda machine was already turning him into a national hero. A cult of hero-worship began to grow around him, which Immelmann – as his personal letters show – found by no means abhorrent. By nature unsociable, arrogant and somewhat petulant, he had in the past taken a good deal of ribbing from his fellow officers because of his dislike of alcohol and indifference to women; now, suddenly, he found himself head and shoulders above the rest, a star in his own element.

Whereas most of his colleagues regarded air combat as a sport, Immelmann approached it from the scientific standpoint, evolving new tactics and improving his efficiency as his experience grew. He developed a new combat manœuvre which was to remain standard in the air fighting textbooks for many years: the Immelmann Turn. This involved building up speed in a dive towards the enemy, then pulling up into a climb and opening fire from below in order to gain surprise. After firing the Fokker pilot continued to climb until he was in the near-vertical position, at which point he applied hard rudder, stall-turned and dived on his adversary from the opposite direction. These tactics worked well as long as the Fokker was superior to all other aircraft at the front; they later became dangerous when more powerful engines enabled Allied aircraft to climb hard after the attacking German fighters and open fire when the latter were at the critical stall-turn position.

Apart from the development of fighting tactics, Immelmann strove constantly to improve his marksmanship. In

7

gaining his first victory he used up some 500 rounds of ammunition in a fight lasting ten minutes; he scored his sixth victory, in November 1915, at a cost of only fifty rounds, many of which found their mark in the bodies of the English pilot and observer, and the ammunition he used in subsequent air fights rarely exceeded that total. He was never in any doubt about the victories he claimed, and was often critical about the claims of others – including his friend Boelcke. 'He claims to have shot down five enemy machines,' Immelmann wrote in October 1915, 'but one of them landed on its own territory. If I counted all those, I should have at least seven. I only count those which crash or land on our ground, and not those which land behind the enemy's lines.'

In the autumn of 1915 Immelmann visited the aircraft designer Antony Fokker at Schwerin, and the two spent long hours discussing ways of improving the existing Fokker E2 monoplane in which Immelmann and his fellow pilots had scored their early victories. The result was the E3, armed with twin Spandau machine-guns, and Section 62 re-equipped with the new type at the end of the year. A couple of weeks later, on 13 January, Boelcke and Immelmann each destroyed a British aircraft while flying E3s; both were awarded the *Pour le Mérite*, the coveted 'Blue Max' – Germany's highest war decoration. It was Immelmann's eighth victory.

It was not until 3 March 1916 that he scored his ninth, and on the fourteenth of that month he succeeded in destroying two aircraft in a single day – a record at that time. He described his tenth victory in a letter home:

'I took off at noon in company with another Fokker pilot, Lieutenant Mulzer, to keep order in the air further south. Several minutes later I saw our batteries firing on an enemy airman to the south of Arras, so off

I went there. When I arrived, I saw a German biplane and another one about a hundred metres above it. As they were doing one another no harm, I thought the second one must be a German too. Nevertheless, I flew up and finally spotted the cockades. Now for it, I thought, and fired . . . and then, after a few shots, my gun jammed.

'I turned away from him, cleared the gun and made another attack. Mulzer had arrived by then, and he joined in. So now we concentrated our fire on him. I sent out 700 rounds of continuous fire, while Mulzer let off 100. Down he went like a stone into the depths and came to earth at Serre village. Naturally both the inmates were killed and the machine completely wrecked. . . .'

The second victory that day came shortly after 5 pm, when Immelmann and two other pilots took off to intercept five enemy aircraft reported to be heading for Douai. The whole affair proved to be almost ridiculously simple. Immelmann caught up with the enemy aircraft – British BEs – over Arras and selected his target, firing 300 rounds at it. The BE fell away and went into a spin, crashing to the east of Arras.

The German tactics of early 1916 involved individual Fokker pilots quartering sectors of the sky over the front, a procedure that was outlined by Immelmann in another letter home.

'Lieutenant Leffers is further southward (of Douai). Bapaume, where I have been busy so often, belongs to his sector. Since there is nothing more to be found in our area, one has to poach on the hunting grounds of others. Baron von Althaus is still further southward, and Parscau another bit further on (Verdun). Berthold is further away to the north. So far each of these has shot down four opponents. Our territories are marked off

9

exactly by the trenches. Naturally the artillery shells us if we come within its range. . . .'

Because of their recognized superiority, the Fokker pilots were never deterred from taking on, single-handed, much larger formations of British or French aircraft. On 29 April, for example, Immelmann – during one of his solitary patrols – sighted a group of five Farman biplanes and attacked them without hesitation, shooting down one and damaging two more. The crew of the downed aircraft escaped with their lives, and the pilot later told Immelmann that his observer had 'lost his head completely and not fired a single shot'. This was not an isolated occurrence: such was the state of affairs in 1916 that more than one Allied airman quite literally froze in terror on sighting a Fokker monoplane.

The next day Immelmann shot down his thirteenth victim. This time, both occupants died. But now the Allied pilots were beginning to develop new tactics in a bid to challenge the Fokkers' supremacy, and a couple of days after Immelmann's later exploit Section 62 lost two machines and their crews in air combat. Immelman went on to destroy his fourteenth enemy – a 'kill' which was shared by Lieutenant Mulzer – near Arras on 23 April, but he himself had a very narrow escape on the twenty-fifth, when he encountered a pair of very determined RFC pilots:

'I had a nasty fight in the air today. I took off about 11 am and met two English biplanes southward of Bapaume. I was about 700 metres higher and therefore came up with them very quickly and attacked one. He seemed to heel over after a few shots, but unfortunately I was mistaken. The two worked splendidly together in the course of the fight and put eleven shots into my machine. The petrol tank, the struts on the fuselage, the undercarriage and the propeller were hit. I could only save myself by a nose-dive of 1000 metres. Then at last the two of them left me alone. It was not a nice business. . . .'

On 5 May Section 62 completed its first year in action, during which time its pilots had claimed the destruction of twenty-five enemy aircraft for the loss of only three of their own number. A fortnight later, on the seventeenth, Immelmann shot down his fifteenth victim, a Bristol Scout. The British pilot was intent on attacking a German LVG and saw Immelmann coming up behind him. After firing only thirty rounds, Immelmann saw the Bristol waver and fall away in a spin. An examination of the wreck later showed that the pilot had been killed by a single bullet.

After a few days of heavy rain, the weather over the front once again cleared on 31 May. Early that morning, a report reached Section 62 that seven enemy aircraft were heading towards Bapaume, and Immelmann took off to intercept them together with Lieutenant Mulzer and Corporal Heinemann. They encountered the British aircraft – Vickers FB5s – near Cambrai and immediately went in to the attack. Immelmann fired at one, which went into a steep glide and was subsequently finished off by Mulzer. Closing in on a second Vickers, Immelmann opened fire again – and suddenly all hell was let loose. The Fokker reared up without warning and a fearful vibration jolted the pilot. Instinctively, as the little aircraft hurtled into a dive, Immelmann switched off the fuel and ignition. He pulled out just in time, with the wings creaking alarmingly, and made a forced landing in a meadow. An examination of the damage soon revealed what had happened; the synchronization gear had failed and he had shot off his own propeller, throwing the engine off balance and almost ripping it from its mounting.

In June 1916, while the battle of the Somme raged, the wind of change began to sweep through the German Air Corps. The old Flying Sections were now to be disbanded and replaced by *Jagdstaffeln*, or Fighter Squadrons, in which Germany's best and most experienced pilots were to be banded together. On 13 June Immelmann sadly bade farewell to his comrades of the old Section 62, most of whom were leaving for the eastern front; he, together with Boelcke and several other notable pilots, was to stay behind and form the first of the new squadrons, *Jagdstaffel* 2 (*Jagdstaffel* 1 existing only on paper). The new unit was to be equipped with Halberstadt Scouts, which promised to be superior to any other combat aircraft at the front.

The morning of 18 June brought heavy clouds, but these dispersed towards noon and the front was soon bathed in sunshine. It was not until 5 pm, however, that enemy aircraft were reported crossing the lines; Immelmann and three other pilots took off to intercept and caught up with the British formation near St Quentin. Immelmann succeeded in damaging one machine, but since it came down in British territory it could not be claimed as a victory.

The Fokkers took off again shortly before dusk. This time, Immelmann was flying one of the older E2s, as his own machine was unserviceable. The Germans ran into seven FE2Bs between Loos and Douai and a whirling dogfight developed. Immelmann hit one of the enemy aircraft, which went down to make a forced landing near Lens, then climbed to search for another victim. At that moment, eye-witnesses on the ground saw Immelmann's aircraft stagger in mid-air, oscillate violently and literally fall apart. The wings collapsed and tore away, while the fuselage broke in two. The front half, including cockpit and pilot, dropped like a stone for six thousand feet and thudded into the ground. Immelmann was killed instantly.

Later, the British claimed that Immelmann had been shot down by Second Lieutenant G. S. McCubbin and Corporal J. H. Waller of No. 25 Squadron, flying an FE, but German experts who examined the wreck attributed the ace's death to failure of the interrupter gear, followed by the destruction of the propeller and subsequent break-up of the Fokker's airframe – a tragic repetition of Immelmann's earlier accident. Eye-witness accounts of the aircraft's behaviour before its last plunge seemed to confirm these findings.

Whatever the reason, the Eagle of Lille would claim no more victims. And although others would go on to sur-pass his score several times over, none could lay claim to being a greater master of his aircraft, or a more brilliant tactician. The whole of Germany mourned his passing; he had founded a tradition which the young pilots who had followed him into action were determined to uphold under their new air leaders, foremost among whom per-haps was the only man who had become the insular Immelmann's true friend: Oswald Boelcke.

2 Oswald Boelcke: the Veteran

One day towards the end of August 1914 an Aviatik two-seater observation aircraft touched down on the airfield occupied by *Fliegerabteilung* 13, east of Mons. The twenty-three-year-old pilot, who had only recently been awarded his pilot's certificate, was looking forward to a reunion with his brother Wilhelm, who served as an observer with the same unit.

The pilot's name was Oswald Boelcke. It was a name which, during the two years that followed, was to inspire the admiration and respect of friend and foe alike. For Boelcke, who was to become one of the first 'aces' in the story of air fighting, was to prove himself not only a natural leader of men, but also a superb tactician under whose guidance the Germans would rapidly establish air superiority over Flanders.

The first months of Boelcke's war career were spent in carrying out reconnaissance and artillery spotting duties, and by the end of 1914 the young pilot had made forty-two operational flights. The Aviatiks he flew were unarmed except for the rifles and revolvers carried by the crew, and although there were isolated instances of German and Allied airmen exchanging shots with similar weapons the months wore on without Boelcke making contact with the enemy.

In the spring of 1915, chafing at what he considered to be an increasingly dull and routine task, Boelcke applied for a transfer to *Fliegerabteilung* 62, which was re-equipping with LVG two-seaters. Fitted with a 150 hp engine, the LVG was one of the first German aircraft to have a machine-gun fitted in the observer's cockpit. It was not an ideal machine for air fighting, but while Anthony Fokker worked hard to perfect his single-seat scout designs with its forward-firing machine-gun, the LVG provided the German squadrons with at least a stop-gap means of protecting slow observation aircraft against increasingly aggressive Allied tactics.

Although he had several skirmishes with Allied aircraft during the early summer of 1915, Boelcke's chance to score his first victory did not arise until 6 July. On that brilliant Sunday morning, Boelcke and his observer, Lieutenant Wühlisch – a former hussar officer who still wore his red cavalry uniform under his flying jacket – took off in their LVG to escort a reconnaissance aircraft. As they were climbing towards the front line, Boelcke spotted a French Morane Parasol several thousand feet higher up. Staying low down, Boelcke made use of the patchwork colours of the countryside to camouflage his aircraft until the Frenchman had flown by, then he swung round and began to stalk the enemy, climbing hard after him and keeping in the French observer's blind spot.

After a chase lasting thirty minutes Boelcke was within firing distance. The French crew had still not seen him, and now he cautiously positioned the LVG behind and slightly above his adversary, slowly increasing power and drawing alongside so that Wühlisch, in the rear cockpit, could bring his gun to bear.

When the range closed to fifty yards Wühlisch opened fire, spraying the Morane with bullets. The startled French pilot, the Comte de Beauvicourt, immediately threw his aircraft into a spiral dive. Boelcke clung grimly to him as he dived and twisted in his frantic attempts to escape; Wühlisch kept on firing in short bursts, pausing every now and then to clear a stoppage. The French gunner returned the fire, but his aim was wild and no bullets hit the LVG.

For twenty minutes the two aircraft wheeled across the sky, Boelcke skilfully anticipating every move the Frenchman made. Finally, at 2000 feet, the Morane went into a shallow dive and crashed into a wood. Boelcke landed alongside and arrived at the wreck at the same time as some German soldiers. Both Frenchmen were dead, each shot through several times. By a strange twist of irony, Boelcke learned later that the Morane had come down in an estate owned by de Beauvicourt himself. No one would ever know what memories of former days might have passed through the Comte's mind as he cruised high over his lands in those last, fatal minutes before Boelcke caught up with him.

Boelcke's first victory was the last he would score while flying a two-seater. Shortly afterwards, he took over the first Fokker monoplane to be delivered to Section 62, leaving Max Immelmann to fly the LVG. Boelcke fell in love with the nimble little monoplane at once, recognizing that at last he had a machine that would enable him to develop his tactics to a fine art. The whole secret, he believed, lay in spotting the enemy first – and in making certain that he did not see you until the last moment, as far as this was possible. Using the Fokker's superior rate of climb to good advantage, Boelcke would cruise at 5000 feet or so just inside the German lines, making full use of the natural camouflage offered by the sun, the clouds and their shadows. He had studied every captured Allied machine in minute detail, with special reference to the arc of fire of its defensive weapons, and he knew its blind spots.

Once he sighted an enemy aircraft – which would normally be flying below his own patrol height of 5000 feet – he would manœuvre carefully until the sun was behind him. Then, hidden by the glare, he would come down in a long, shallow dive towards his victim, waiting until he was very close before opening fire in short bursts. As soon as his opponent fell, he would climb rapidly to resume his patrol, rather like a hawk that quartered the sky before stooping to make its kill.

Later, as the Allies adopted more defensive tactics to counter the supremacy of the Fokkers – the RFC escorting its observation aircraft with Vickers fighters and the French drastically reducing the radius of their combat sorties – Boelcke began to cross the front line into Allied territory in search of further victims. It was now, when he began to encounter fighter escorts, that he discovered a basic flaw in his lone-wolf tactics. He could still find enemy aircraft without trouble, but while he was concentrating on his victim he found it impossible to keep a good look-out at the same time, and on more than one occasion he narrowly escaped being taken by surprise when a second Allied machine crept up on him.

The answer, he reasoned, was for the Fokkers to work in pairs. In this way the second Fokker, flying off to one side and some distance behind, could guard the first's tail at all times. So, in the autumn of 1915, Boelcke evolved the concept of the 'pair', the basic air fighting formation that is still used today. And, to form the other half of the pair, he selected from the ranks of Section 62 another young pilot who was busily carving out a reputation for himself: Max Immelmann.

Together, the two made a formidable team during the closing weeks of 1915, when Boelcke was sent to Metz to fly in the Verdun sector. Soon after his arrival, he broke up a formation of French bombers which had just raided

Metz station, shooting down one in flames and driving the others away. This feat was witnessed by the Kaiser, who had just arrived at Metz in a special train to make a tour of the German positions.

In January 1916 Boelcke and Immelmann each scored their eighth victories and were awarded the *Ordre Pour le Mérite*. Almost all Boelcke's victories so far had been against the French, whereas Immelmann, who was based at Douai, continued to make his mark against the British. Skilful and ruthlessly efficient though he was in air combat, Boelcke derived no pleasure from killing; he felt genuine compassion for the airmen he shot down, and whenever possible he visited wounded adversaries in hospital, laden with gifts.

The friendly rivalry between Immelmann and Boelcke continued throughout the spring of 1916, ending only with Immelmann's death in June. By this time Boelcke had scored eighteen victories, and the Kaiser, profoundly shocked by the news that Immelmann had fallen, ordered Boelcke to take a rest. He was to go to Turkey, Germany's ally, to make a goodwill tour of the air squadrons serving on that front.

In July, while his tour was in full swing, he received an urgent message from Berlin. The British, it said, had launched a massive offensive on the Somme, and the Royal Flying Corps, which had reorganized its fighter squadrons, had managed to establish air superiority over the battlefield.

Boelcke was to return to France immediately and organize a new Jagdstaffel of fourteen fighters, which would be flown by the best pilots available. Boelcke was to select them personally. The *Jagdstaffel* would be positioned in opposition to the RFC's best units, so it could expect some heavy fighting. Boelcke, conscious that time was of the utmost importance, began his selection among the personnel of German air units on the eastern front, which he visited on his way back to Germany. The first two men he picked were both, in their own ways, to have a profound influence on the course of the air war on the western front. One was Lieutenant Erwin Boehme – a man far older, at the age of thirty-seven, than the average pilot, but whose reliability and sound common sense would be useful in training younger and more headstrong men. The other was a slim young Prussian named Manfred von Richthofen.

The initial base chosen for Boelcke's new unit, *Jagdstaffel* 2, was Lagnicourt, which lay in a rear area in the Somme sector. His eager young pilots began to assemble there at the beginning of August, but the equipment he had been promised – the new Albatros DII fighter, with its twin Spandau machine-guns firing through the propeller – was slower to arrive. By the second week in August *Jagdstaffel* 2 still had only three of these machines, so Boelcke flew a Fokker in combat while his students trained to operational efficiency on the Albatros. Boelcke's absence had in no way impaired his skill, as he demonstrated by shooting down two more enemy machines before the end of the month. The aircraft flown by the ace while scoring these victories was the new Fokker DII biplane, which, like the Albatros, was armed with twin Spandaus.

Time and again, when talking to his students, Boelcke hammered home the lesson that it was by no means sufficient just to be a good pilot. They had to know everything about their aircraft: its combat radius, its maximum and cruising speeds at various altitudes, what stresses it could sustain in violent manœuvres, and so on. He made them strip engines and put them together again, so that they could carry out temporary repairs if they had to make a forced landing with engine trouble. He also instructed them on the finer points of shooting, stressing that it was always better to get in close and fire in short bursts, aiming for the cockpit. He taught them how to maintain their machine-guns with loving care, and how to clear stoppages quickly while still exercising full control over the aircraft.

He taught them the value of teamwork and of keeping a good look-out at all times. The day of the lone hunter, he pointed out, was over. He allocated formation positions to his pilots so that they would get used to having the same wingman alongside, and painted the nose and tail of his own aircraft red so that it would be easily recognizable in the mêlée of a dogfight, or when his pilots were forming up over a rendezvous. If the formation got broken up in the course of a scrap, the pilots were to make for one of a series of rendezvous points selected by Boelcke. If no one else turned up, individual pilots were to go home, keeping just below cloud cover if possible to reduce the risk of being attacked from above.

During the first two weeks of September, while his young men trained, Boelcke continued to fight and score victories. Despite their repeated entreaties, he refused to release his pilots – his 'cubs', as he affectionately called them – for operational flying until he was certain that they had reached peak efficiency.

That day finally came on 17 September, when Boelcke led his Jagdstaffel into action as a team for the first time. On that Sunday morning, accompanied by five of his pilots, he encountered eight BE2cs of No. 12 Squadron RFC, escorted by six FE2bs, on their way to attack the railway station at Marcoing. Boelcke attacked just as the BEs were releasing their bombs, after positioning his fighters across the British machines' avenue of escape. In the ensuing battle, two BEs and four of their escorts were shot down, one of the latter by von Richthofen.

This success provided tremendous encouragement not only for Boelcke's fledgelings but also for other German units which were going into action. During the weeks that followed, air superiority took a marked swing back in the Germans' favour. Throughout these weeks, Boelcke's *staffel* remained at the core of the German air defence, its pilots scoring a combined total of twenty-seven victories in the last fortnight of September alone. The cost to themselves was three aircraft.

The RFC hit back, attacking Boelcke's base at Lagnicourt furiously and obliging *Jagdstaffel* 2 to move to another location, but the British losses continued to mount. The German fighter strength was growing all the time as new *staffeln* reached the front, and by the middle of October it stood at over 300 machines.

A spell of bad weather beginning on 22 October brought some respite, but on the twenty-sixth Boelcke was airborne again with eight of his fighters, harassing British observation aircraft over Ancre. Three were shot down, together with a Nieuport Scout. This new success brought Boelcke's personal score to forty aircraft destroyed – half of them within the space of two months.

On the morning of the twenty-eighth, when Boelcke next flew, the RFC seemed to be taking a day off. He and his men carried out four sorties without sighting a single enemy aircraft. Boelcke, in fact, was not sorry about the lack of action; the strain of combat was beginning to tell, as he had remarked to Erwin Boehme the day before. The two men, who had become close friends, had spent the previous evening listening to gramophone records before going to bed early.

Then, in the afternoon, came a call for assistance from a German position at the front, which was being attacked. Boelcke immediately took off, accompanied by von Richthofen, Boehme and three other pilots. They soon sighted their quarry; two de Havilland Scouts of No. 24 Squadron RFC, patrolling just above the clouds.

As Boelcke started his attack, six more German fighters arrived and also dived on the two de Havillands, which began turning for their lives. In the midst of the mêlée, Boelcke and Boehme headed for the same de Havilland. Neither German pilot saw the other. The next instant, Boehme felt a sudden jolt. His undercarriage had struck Boelcke's wing-tip, tearing it away.

The battle was abandoned and the two de Havillands, forgotten now, made their escape as the Germans milled around and watched Boelcke's stricken machine descend in wide spirals. It appeared that he still had some measure of control. Then it dropped into a thin layer of cloud, and when it re-emerged it was spinning; the whole of the damaged wing had broken away. Boelcke was killed on impact.

Erwin Boehme was inconsolable. In fact, he would have shot himself had von Richthofen not intervened and convinced him that Boelcke would not have wished it. Boehme went on flying, scoring twenty-four victories before he was shot down on 29 November 1917 by Captain John Pattern of No. 10 Squadron, RFC.

Boelcke was dead, but the lessons of air combat he had driven home were not forgotten. In 1917 his 'cubs', now full-grown wolves, would write those lessons in blood and fire across the sky of Flanders.

The day after he died, a British aircraft flew over the German lines and dropped a wreath, together with a message. It read: 'To the memory of Captain Boelcke, our brave and chivalrous opponent.'

There could have been no finer or more sincere tribute.

3 Werner Voss: the 'Flying Hussar'

The Albatros Scout cruised high over the front line, its young pilot anxiously scanning the drab, churned-up earth beneath for the tell-tale flicker of movement that would betray the presence of an Allied reconnaissance aircraft. It was several weeks now since he had joined the famous 'Boelcke' *Jagdstaffel* 2, and he had yet to score his first victory – a fact that caused him some frustration, surrounded as he was by some of Germany's top fighter pilots.

Now, on this morning of 27 November, he was to have his chance at last. Just as he was about to go home, he sighted an unsuspecting BE2c, a couple of thousand feet lower down. Diving to the attack, he opened fire and saw his bullets ripping into the BE's wings. The aircraft went into a fast descent, its pilot apparently intent on getting down in one piece before the German shot him out of the sky, and made a crash landing in no-man's land quite close to the British lines. The British pilot and observer jumped from the cockpit and ran to the safety of their own trenches.

The German pilot circled overhead, raging. Since the BE had come down outside German territory, there was no way of claiming it as a 'kill'; the German infantry who had occupied that particular sector had pulled out early that morning, and consequently there would be no witnesses. Quickly, the young German made up his mind. Throttling back, he glided down to land among the shell craters and came to a stop a few yards from the wreck of the British machine. Jumping down, he ran through the clinging mud and scrambled on to the BE's splintered wing, reaching into the rear cockpit and pulling the machine-gun from its mounting. Burdened by his trophy, he stumbled back to his own aircraft and threw himself into his seat. Mud sprayed up behind the wheels as he opened the throttle. Bullets crackled around him as the Albatros lurched into the air, but miraculously none struck home. That night, the machine-gun was mounted in the officers' mess of *Jagdstaffel* 2, and Lieutenant Werner Voss was officially credited with his first victory.

It is perhaps no exaggeration to claim that the men of the Royal Flying Corps held Werner Voss in greater esteem than any other German pilot they encountered in action over Flanders between 1916 and 1918. He enjoyed a meteoric rise to fame; his fighting career lasted barely ten months, but in that time he was to destroy forty-eight enemy aircraft and assure himself of a place among the ranks of the greatest fighter pilots of all time.

Born in 1897, Voss, like many other young men who were to make a name for themselves in the German Flying Corps, first saw military service in a cavalry regiment, a fact that later earned him the nickname 'the Hussar of Krefeld'. In 1915 however, while Voss was still only eighteen, he succeeded in gaining a transfer to the Imperial German Air Service, where he served initially as an observer. The routine, if sometimes highly dangerous, task of artillery observation failed to arouse much enthusiasm in the young ex-hussar, and after a few weeks of it he applied for pilot training, intent on single-seat flying.

The summer of 1916 found him undergoing his flying training course, during which he showed considerable aptitude. His instructors soon recognized his potential as a single-seater pilot, and in the autumn of 1916, having completed his course successfully, he was posted to the élite *Jagdstaffel* 2. His first success, the BE2c forced down on 27 November, was followed quickly by another; the next day he accounted for a Nieuport Scout. However, it was to be well into the new year before he claimed any further victims; but then, in the seven weeks between 1 February and 24 March 1917, he shot down no fewer than nineteen Allied aircraft, placing himself firmly among the ranks of the German aces and bringing the total number of kills scored by *Jagdstaffel* 2 since its formation to 120.

In April 1917 Voss was one of the small band of top-ranking German pilots selected to test the latest of Anthony Fokker's fighter designs: the DRI triplane. Voss knew instinctively, when he took the triplane up for the first time, that the nimble little fighter was a thoroughbred; its top speed of 113 mph, its high degree of manœuvrability and its armament of two Spandau machine-guns would give it the edge over the Allied fighter types which were coming into service to challenge the supremacy of the earlier Fokker and Albatros machines.

It would be several weeks before the DRI reached the front-line squadrons, however, and in the meantime Voss was given a Staffel of his own, equipped with Albatros DVs. Like many other German pilots of this period, Voss adopted his own personal colour scheme. This varied from aircraft to aircraft, and included red wings and tail accompanied by a checkerboard design on the fuselage as well as a pale green overall finish. The most usual scheme, however – and the one that became most familiar to the Allied pilots who encountered him – was all black, with a white skull and crossbones design painted on either side of the fuselage.

By the end of July 1917 Voss's score had risen to thirty. A few days later his squadron re-equipped with Fokker triplanes, and in the first ten days of August the German destroyed five more Allied machines while flying this type of aircraft. He accounted for a further four aircraft before the end of the month, and in September he demonstrated his prowess still further by achieving a series of multiple victories. On the morning of the fifth he shot down a Sopwith Pup, and later that day destroyed a French Caudron reconnaissance aircraft. Five days later, he surprised a formation of three Sopwith Camels, shot down one with his first firing pass, put a burst into another which broke up in mid-air, and chased the third until it made its escape across the British lines. Continuing his patrol, he sighted an FE2d and attacked it; the wings tore off the British biplane and its debris fluttered down to crash in no-man's land.

The following day Voss destroyed two more Allied aircraft, bringing his score to forty-seven. It was his last taste of action for a fortnight; his superiors, recognizing that the strain of continual combat was beginning to tell on him, sent him home for a well-earned rest. During the next few days he spent a lot of time in the company of Anthony Fokker, whose parties had become legendary among pilots on leave; several others were there too, including the celebrated von Richthofen, who by this time had scored sixty victories and who was recovering from a head wound.

Voss had no scruples about living life to the full, and he was nursing a mighty hangover on his return to the bosom of *Jagdstaffel* 10 on 23 September. The night before, at a party thrown by Fokker at the Bristol Hotel on Berlin's Unter den Linden, a fellow Staffel leader, Bruno Loerzer, had been awarded the *Pour le Mérite* – Germany's highest decoration for valour, popularly known as the 'Blue Max'. The champagne and wine had flown freely, and Voss had been one of the last to leave the bar.

Nevertheless, a couple of hours after his return he was in the air, searching for another victim. He soon found it; a de Havilland DH4, heading back towards the British lines. The British pilot saw the menace on his tail and tried to reach friendly territory in a long dive, but Voss's first burst killed his gunner and within seconds his aircraft was spiralling down in flames.

On the way back to his airfield Voss experienced some engine trouble, so that he turned his aircraft over to the mechanics and got another machine ready for his next sortie. It was similar to his own in every respect apart from the colour scheme, which was silver-blue with a red nose. At 6 pm the same day, despite poor visibility, he took off in this aircraft to carry out a lone patrol over the British lines. He had set himself a target; he would try and 'bag' two more Allied aircraft before dusk, to bring his score up to fifty.

Soon after starting his patrol, he spotted a likely victim; a solitary SE5, flying eastwards. A quick look round told Voss that no other enemy aircraft were in the vicinity and he began his dive towards the SE. In another minute, if all went well, the British airman would become Voss's forty-ninth kill.

Twenty minutes earlier, six SE5s of 'B' Flight, No. 56 Squadron Royal Flying Corps, had taken off from their base a few miles on the other side of the lines to carry out an offensive patrol. Almost as soon as the SEs arrived over the front, their leader, Captain James McCudden, had spotted an enemy two-seater and attacked it, sending it down in flames. Re-forming his flight immediately, he then climbed hard to intercept a formation of six Albatros Scouts, slipping along just under the cloud base.

At that moment, McCudden sighted the lone SE fleeing for its life, with Voss in hot pursuit. Abandoning the Albatros formation he went after the silver-blue triplane in a diving turn, accompanied by one of his pilots, Lieutenant Albert Rhys-Davids. The pair closed in rapidly on the German, one on either side, and began to open fire in short bursts.

Voss, alerted by the first rattle of gun-fire behind him, must have sized up his situation in an instant. The SE5s were faster than his triplane, so that any attempt to get away by diving was out of the question. Neither would he have much of a chance if he tried to climb, for a flight of Spads had arrived and were now circling overhead, sparring with and holding off the Albatros formation. With the other four SE's coming down fast to join McCudden and Rhys-Davids, Voss took the only course open to him. He decided to turn and fight, hoping that the Fokker's manœuvrability would enable him to hold his own until reinforcements arrived.

McCudden signalled to Rhys-Davids and the two SEs spread out, trying to box in the triplane. Voss, however, was far too experienced to be caught out like that. Abandoning the SE he had been chasing, he stood the triplane on its wing-tip and pulled round in a steep turn to face his attackers, firing as he came. McCudden, taken completely by surprise, took the first burst through his SEs wings and broke away sharply. At that moment, a red-nosed Albatros DV, which had managed to break through the cordon of Spads up above, arriving like a thunderbolt and joined in the fray. Its pilot was almost as skilful as Voss himself. He undertook the task of protecting Voss's tail, and with his assistance the German ace abandoned his purely defensive tactics and got in some damaging shots at the SEs that were desperately trying to out-turn him.

For ten minutes the six SEs and the two German machines gyrated around the sky, the Germans looking out all the while for the expected help that would enable them to escape. It never came, and the outcome was inevitable. The combat report of Lieutenant Rhys-Davids described the last frantic minutes of the fight:

'The red-nosed Albatros and the triplane fought magnificently. I got in several bursts at the triplane without apparent effect, and twice placed a new drum on my Lewis gun. Eventually I got east of and slightly above the triplane and made for it, getting in a whole Lewis drum and a corresponding number of rounds from my Vickers. He made an attempt to turn in and we were so close that I was certain that we would collide. He passed my starboard wing by inches and went down. I zoomed, and saw him next with his engine apparently out, gliding east. I dived again and got one shot out of my Vickers. I reloaded, keeping in the dive, and got in another good burst, the triplane effecting a slight starboard turn, still going down. I had now overshot him, zoomed, but never saw him again.'

McCudden, having broken off the fight for the moment to change an ammunition drum, saw the triplane's last moments. It seemed to stagger and fly erratically for a few moments; then it went into a steep dive, streaming smoke, and exploded on impact with the ground. An instant later it was joined by the red-nosed Albatros, torn apart by the other SEs. The burning wreckage of both aircraft glowed brightly in the gathering dusk as the SEs formed up and headed for home.

That night, No. 56 Squadron's mess was full of discussion about the desperate fight. As yet, the British pilots were unaware of the German pilot's identity. Then the news came through. The wrecked Fokker had been found, and on the uniform of its pilot was the insignia of the Boelcke *Jagdgeschwader* and the star of the *Pour le Merite*. The word spread through the Allied ranks like wildfire: the legendary Werner Voss was dead.

Later, James McCudden was to write of him: 'His flying was wonderful, his courage magnificent, and in my opinion he was the bravest German airman whom it has been my privilege to see fight.'

Perhaps the feelings of the British pilots were best summed up by young Rhys-Davids himself, the man who had ended Voss's life. As his colleagues gathered round to congratulate him, he shook his head sadly and murmured, as he set his glass aside:

'Oh, if only I could have brought him down alive!'

4 Manfred von Richthofen: the Red Knight of Germany

It was 21 April 1918. After four weeks of almost continual retreat the Allied armies had at last halted the final great German offensive of the war, having broken its back with the use of air power on an unprecedented scale, and were now counter-attacking all along the front. For the hundreds of thousands of British and French soldiers and airmen on the western front, the twenty-first dawned with no promise of being any different from the days before it; days characterized by bitter, bloody fighting, but days nevertheless of no special significance except to those whose lives ended brutally in a crackle of bullets or crash of shells.

Yet before this day ended, it was to assume very special significance indeed to millions on both sides of the front. For 21 April 1918 was the day the Baron died.

Shortly after 10 am on that April day, Baron Manfred von Richthofen strolled across the dew-studded grass of Cappy airfield, savouring the crisp breeze that blew from the east. In spite of a somewhat riotous party the night before – in celebration of his eightieth victory – the quiet, twenty-five-year-old pilot felt fit and well. He was looking forward to a spell of leave, which he planned to spend hunting with some friends in the Black Forest, far away from the howl of tortured engines and the chatter of machine-guns.

But that was still several days away, and in the meantime, with the German air squadrons operating at full stride in support of the increasingly hard-pressed field armies, there was much work to be done. Today, von Richthofen would be leading two squadrons of fighters on patrol over the front line.

The Baron walked towards his scarlet-painted Fokker triplane. By his side trotted his black labrador, Moritz. Suddenly, an airman pointed a camera at him. Most German pilots believed it unlucky to be photographed just before a flight, but von Richthofen laughed at such superstitions. He smiled as he turned to face the camera. The shutter clicked, and von Richthofen was photographed – for the last time.

As he was about to climb into his aircraft, another airman came up to him with a postcard he wanted to send to his son. He asked the pilot to sign it. 'What's the matter,' asked von Richthofen, smiling. 'Don't you think I'll come back?' He signed his name – for the last time.

Twenty miles away, at Bertangles aerodrome on the other side of the lines, the Sopwith Camels of No. 209 Squadron, Royal Air Force, were revving up their engines. The pilots had not yet had time to take in the fact that, three weeks earlier, the Royal Flying Corps had ceased to exist and the RAF was born in its place; they had been too busy fighting. In the cockpit of one of the fighters sat twenty-four-year-old, Canadian-born Captain Roy Brown. A veteran pilot with the DSC and twelve kills to his credit, Brown presented a very different picture from von Richthofen. Battle fatigue had taken its toll and had turned him into an old man. His face was sallow, and a nerve twitched at the corner of his mouth. He lived on brandy and milk, his tortured stomach constantly rejecting solid food. He gripped the joystick hard, desperately trying to stop his hand trembling. He felt sick and miserable. Yet this young, nerve-shattered man was soon to earn himself a place in history. Within half an hour, he would meet Manfred von Richthofen in combat two miles above the ground in a duel that would leave only one survivor....

Von Richthofen had joined the German Flying Corps in May 1915, after spending the first months of the war in action with the 1st Regiment of Uhlans. During the summer of 1915 he flew as an observer on both eastern and western fronts, and during the Champagne battle in September he shot down his first enemy aircraft, a Farman two-seater. Since the Farman came down on French territory, however, von Richthofen was unable to claim credit for it.

Soon afterwards he was accepted for pilot training, going solo for the first time on 10 October 1915. The following March, having successfully completed his course, he joined a two-seater unit in the Verdun sector, and in April he shot down a Nieuport – although this, too, fell behind the French lines and could not be claimed. There were more skirmishes during the weeks that followed, but von Richthofen had yet to win his first official victory when, in June, his squadron was suddenly transferred to the eastern front to carry out bombing and reconnaissance duties.

It was still there in August, when the awed pilots received a visit from the great Oswald Boelcke, on his way back to France after a trip to Turkey. Boelcke, who had received orders to form a *Jagdstaffel*, was on the look-out for talent, and von Richthofen – who had met Boelcke once before, on a train – soon pushed himself forward. Despite von Richthofen's poor record at flying school, Boelcke recognized enthusiasm when he saw it, and the young pilot had certainly showed prowess while flying the unwieldly AVG two-seater. To von Richthofen's delight, he was invited to join Boelcke's embryo squadron on the Somme.

It was not long before Boelcke learned that his choice had been fully justified. On 17 September he selected four pilots – including von Richthofen – to accompany him on an offensive patrol. It was *Jagdstaffel* 2's first war flight as a team, using its new Albatros Scouts. Over the front, the Germans encountered a British formation consisting of eight bomb-carrying BE2cs escorted by six FE2b two-seater scouts. After stalking the British for some distance, Boelcke led his pilots into the attack. Von Richthofen, after making one ill-judged firing pass during which he almost came to grief, remembered what Boelcke had taught him and made another approach, creeping in beneath his opponent in the British observer's blind spot. When the range was close enough he opened fire, raking the FE's underside from nose to tail. His bullets shattered the FE's engine and mortally wounded both observer and pilot. The latter, retaining a measure of control, made a successful forced landing. Von Richthofen, unable to restrain himself, landed alongside and reached the British aircraft just as German soldiers were lifting out the blood-stained bodies of the two airmen. The observer opened his eyes as von Richthofen bent over him, smiled, and died. The pilot was rushed to a nearby dressing station, but was dead on arrival. Somewhat sobered, von Richthofen climbed into his Albatros and flew back to *Jagdstaffel* 2's base at Lagnicourt.

That same night, von Richthofen wrote to a jeweller he knew in Berlin and asked him to send a small silver cup, two inches high, engraved with the date and the type of aircraft von Richthofen had shot down. The jeweller did as he was asked, never dreaming that in the course of the next two years he would be called upon to furnish no fewer than eighty similar trophies.

Boelcke's untimely death in October 1916 made the young pilots he had nurtured fiercely determined to carry on his tradition, and with the training he had given them some of their individual scores began to mount quickly – so quickly, in fact, that bets were laid on the date when Boelcke's final tally of forty would be surpassed. By the middle of November von Richthofen's score stood at thirteen – and there it nearly stopped, for a few days later, on the twenty-third, he had the toughest air battle of his career and came very close to losing it.

His opponent was the leading R F C ace of the day, Major Lanoe George Hawker, VC, DSO. An experienced pilot who had learned to fly before the war, Hawker had first achieved fame by bombing the German Zeppelin sheds at Cologne from a height of only 200 feet. Later, he had become the first pilot to destroy three enemy aircraft in a single day, a feat that earned him his Victoria Cross. Von Richthofen encountered Hawker when the latter, flying with two other machines, detached himself and dived on the German, who was flying alone. Later, von Richthofen described the ensuing fight in his diary:

'The Englishman tried to catch me up in the rear while I tried to get behind him. So we circled round and round like madmen after one another at an altitude of about 10,000 feet. First we circled twenty times to the left, and then thirty times to the right. Each tried to get behind and above the other....

'When we had got down to about 6000 feet without having achieved anything particular, my opponent ought to have discovered that it was time for him to take his leave. The wind was favourable for me, for it drove us more and more towards the German positions. At last we were above Bapaume, about half a mile behind the German front. The gallant fellow was full of pluck, and when we had got down to about 3000 feet he merrily waved to me as if to say, Well, how do you do?

'The circles which we made around one another were so narrow that their diameter was probably no more than 250 or 300 feet. I had time to take a good look at my opponent. I looked down into his carriage and could see every movement of his head. If he had not had his helmet on I would have seen what kind of face he was making.

'My Englishman was a good sportsman, but by and by the thing became a little too hot for him. He had to decide whether he would land on German ground or whether he would fly back to the English lines. Of course he tried the latter, after having endeavoured in vain to escape me by loopings and such tricks. At that time his first bullets were flying around me, for so far neither of us had been able to do any shooting. When he had come down to about 300 feet he tried to escape by flying a zig-zag course, which makes it difficult for an observer on the ground to shoot. That was my most favourable moment. I followed him at an altitude of from 250 feet to 150 feet, firing all the time. The English-men could not help falling. But the jamming of my gun nearly robbed me of success.

'My opponent fell shot through the head 150 feet behind our lines. His machine-gun was dug out of the ground and it ornaments the entrance of my dwelling....'

At the end of the year Richthofen, who had now de-stroyed sixteen aircraft, was given command of his own squadron, *Jagdstaffel* 11. The fact did not especially please him, as he recorded: 'I must say I was annoyed. I had learnt to work so well with my comrades of Boelcke's squadron, and now I had to begin all over again working hand in hand with different people. It was a beastly nuisance.' Nevertheless, his annoyance was tempered a few days later by the news that he had been awarded the *Pour le Mérite.*

Now that he was in command of his own unit, and consequently in a position to authorize all flights himself, von Richthofen flew at every available opportunity. His score increased by leaps and bounds, as did his self-confidence; the latter was shaken slightly in March 1917, when his fuel tank was holed at 9000 feet and he glided down to make a forced landing, expecting to burst into flames all the while, but he was soon back in action again and by the end of the month his score stood at thirty-one.

During 'Bloody April' of 1917, when the RFC suffered terrible losses in the Arras sector, von Richthofen – conspicuous in his scarlet-painted Albatros – seemed to be everywhere along the front. The pilots of *Jagdstaffel* 11 followed his example and painted their machines in garish colours, advertising their presence to their opponents in a gesture that was almost one of supreme contempt.

In the first week of April alone, the RFC lost seventy-five aircraft in combat – victims of an emerging band of tough, resolute German air fighters nurtured in the traditions of Boelcke and Immelmann, men who had a superlative weapon in the Albatros and whose teamwork was excellent. At the head of the team was von Richthofen, but close behind him came a host of other redoubtable German pilots: men like Bruno Loerzer, the leader of *Jagdstaffel* 26, who shot down ten British aircraft during the Battle of Arras and who was to end the war with forty-five victories; the formidable Werner Voss; Erich Lowenhardt, who had forty victories in the spring of 1917 and who went on to score sixteen more; Karl Allmenroeder and Karl Schaefer, with thirty victories each; Kurt Wolff, with twenty-seven at the time of the Battle of Arras; Otto Bernert with twenty-six; and many others who were to be included in the list of Germany's fifty top-scorers by the end of the war.

Since the German practice was to concentrate their best pilots in crack units, most of these men served in von Richthofen's *Jagdstaffel* 11 at one time or another before going on to commands of their own. During the fighting of April 1917 von Richthofen's unit was expanded into a *Jagdgeschwader* (Fighter Wing) of three squadrons, a highly mobile formation that could be switched rapidly from one sector to another, wherever it was most needed. It was not long before it became known, in the popular press at least, as 'Richthofen's Flying Circus'.

The RFC went to considerable lengths in their efforts to whittle down the overall German superiority, concentrating their best squadrons in opposition to von Richthofen wherever he appeared. So long as the Albatros remained superior to the British fighter types, however, the challenge to von Richthofen could never be a serious one, and new equipment was eagerly awaited. When No. 48 Squadron RFC received six new Bristol Fighters – powerful two-seat machines fitted with Rolls-Royce engines and armed with three guns – hopes ran high that they would form the vanguard of real resistance to the Red Baron. But the Bristols were rushed into action before their pilots had become used to them, and their first brush with von Richthofen was a disaster; four were shot down and the other two limped back to base with severe damage. In his subsequent report, von Richthofen said that the Bristol Fighter was inferior to the Albatros – a statement that was unwittingly to sign the death warrant of many German airmen who failed to appreciate that the Bristol, in the hands of an experienced pilot, could be a very deadly opponent.

It was with considerable relief that the RFC, sadly depleted by the spring battles, learned that von Richthofen had been slightly wounded and put out of action for a time early in July. It had happened on the sixth, when forty fighters of the Richthofen Geschwader attacked six FE2ds of No. 20 Squadron, escorted by four Sopwith Triplanes of No. 10 Squadron, Royal Naval Air Service. Two FEs were shot down, but an observer in another – 2nd Lieutenant A. E. Woodbridge – got in a good burst at von Richthofen's red Albatros and sent it down to make a forced landing. Von Richthofen was wounded in the head.

Because of his injury he missed the start of the next major period of air action. The third battle of Ypres opened on 11 July, and on that day fourteen German aircraft were shot down for the loss of nine British. Squadrons of the R F C were now starting to re-equip with a formidable new fighter, the Sopwith Camel, and now it was the turn of the *Jagdstaffeln* to suffer. A few days later von Richthofen, concerned by the growing losses of the German squadrons, returned to the front with his head still swathed in bandages. During the last days of July his *Jagdgeschwader* – now consisting of *Jagdstaffeln* 4, 6, 10 and 11 – took part in a series of massive dogfights with Allied fighter formations. On the twenty-sixth, for example, no fewer than ninety-four single-seat fighters fought one another in a desperate battle over Polygon Wood.

In August 1917 the *Richthofen Geschwader* re-equipped with Fokker triplanes, which once again enabled it to hold its own against the ever-growing number of Camel squadrons. By the end of the year the *Geschwader*'s strength had increased to five *staffeln* – about sixty aircraft – and the morale and efficiency of its pilots remained as high as ever. Von Richthofen's personal score now stood at sixty-three, and he was the idol of Germany; the cult that grew around him far overshadowed the hero-worship that had surrounded Boelcke and Immelmann.

Von Richthofen's rules for air fighting were simple enough. 'Never shoot holes in a machine,' was his dictum. 'Aim for the man and don't miss him. If you are fighting a two-seater, get the observer first; until you have silenced the gun don't bother about the pilot.' He followed his own advice with ruthless efficiency; there were bullet-holes in the bodies of most of his victims.

He brought the same kind of ruthless approach to the training of new pilots. Having satisfied himself that a replacement could handle a Fokker competently, he would literally throw him in at the deep end, ordering him to go off and shoot down an Englishman. Some young pilots inevitably failed to return from these lone sorties; those who did come back had learned more about air fighting in an hour than weeks of practice could have taught them.

Although his prowess in the air remained undiminished, a marked change came over von Richthofen during the early weeks of 1918. A lone wolf at the best of times – a fact that made his superlative grasp of teamwork and tactics even more remarkable – he took to spending more and more time on his own, retiring to his room early in the evening to be alone with his thoughts. Friends noted that he seemed to become obsessed with the idea of death by fire, commenting on the number of his opponents who went down in flames. He never showed any outward signs of fear that this might one day be his fate – but no one knew what private nightmares he suffered when he shut himself into his room.

By the middle of April 1918 von Richthofen's official score had risen to eighty. Bearing in mind the German system of crediting victories, the actual total may have been considerably higher. Now, on the twenty-first, the Baron had every intention of pushing the total well towards the ninety mark before departing on leave in three days' time.

At 10.45 am von Richthofen's fifteen brightly-painted Fokker triplanes droned steadily westwards, high above the valley of the Somme. It was not long before the pilots sighted their first enemy; two lumbering British RE8 reconnaissance aircraft, photographing the German trenches. Four of the German fighters broke away and sped down to the attack, ignoring a curtain of shell-bursts thrown up by the British anti-aircraft guns.

A couple of miles away, Captain Roy Brown saw the white puffs of the shells and an instant later picked out the flashing wings of the enemy fighters. He immediately led the eight Camels of 209 Squadron to the rescue of the hard-pressed REs, and soon the sky was filled with whirling aircraft as the remainder of the Fokkers, which had been circling watchfully overhead, came tumbling down like an avalanche and joined the fray.

One of the Camel pilots was seeing action for the first time. He was Lieutenant Wilfred R. May, and he was an old school chum of Brown's. The latter had told him not to get mixed up in the general dogfight, but to hang around on the fringe and get in a shot if the chance presented itself. Now, as he watched the battle develop, the excited May saw a Fokker that looked like a sitting target and dived after it. He closed in rapidly and opened fire, missing his target by a hopeless margin. As he tried desperately to correct his aim, his guns suddenly jammed; in his enthusiasm he had kept his finger on the triggers for too long. Swearing, he broke off the chase and dived away towards home, once again obeying Brown's instructions.

From his vantage point above the mêlée, von Richthofen had seen the lone Camel break away. It was just the moment he had been waiting for. Putting his triplane into a shallow dive, he positioned himself on May's tail and gradually overhauled the British aircraft. Up above, Lieutenant Hans Wolff, who had set himself the task of guarding von Richthofen's tail at all times, was alarmed on seeing his leader dive towards the British lines and prepared to go after him. Just then, however, he was compelled to take evasive action when a Camel attacked him. There was no sign of the red triplane when he looked again.

The first hint May had of the danger on his tail was the rattle of von Richthofen's machine-guns. Twisting in his seat, he felt sick horror as he saw the red triplane only yards behind, the black helmeted head of its pilot clearly visible behind the gun-sight. Instinctively, he kicked on hard rudder and pushed the stick over, sending the Camel skidding across the sky in a steep turn, but his pursuer clung grimly to him.

High above, Brown – who had been mixed up in a nightmare merry-go-round with half a dozen enemy fighters – suddenly found himself alone. Glancing down, he saw May's Camel and the red triplane twisting and weaving along the Somme Valley. Without hesitation, he dived down to his friend's aid.

By this time, May was practically exhausted. He had tried everything to shake off his deadly pursuer, and every move had failed. Von Richthofen kept on firing in short bursts, his bullets ripping through the Camel's wings and sending up flurries of spray from the river. The speeding aircraft were down to less than 200 feet now, skimming the surface of the Somme.

'Just near Corbie,' May said later, 'von Richthofen beat me to it and came over the hill. At that point I was a sitting duck; I was too low down between the banks to make a turn away from him. I felt that he had me cold, and I was in such a state of mind at this time that I had to restrain myself from pushing the stick forward and diving into the river, as I knew that I had had it.'

Brown arrived just in time, pulling out of his dive above and slightly to the right of the Fokker. Correcting with rudder, he got the red triplane squarely in his sights and opened fire with his twin Vickers. Bullets sewed a trail of holes along the triplane's fuselage. Von Richthofen looked round, and Brown clearly saw what seemed to be an expression of startled horror on his face beneath the goggles. Then he slumped sideways in the cockpit. The Fokker swerved violently, then righted itself and nosed over into a glide. It hit the ground and bounced, shedding a wheel, then slid to a halt the right way up two miles inside the British lines, close to some Australian trenches.

Not only Brown had fired at von Richthofen. Near Corbie, two Australians of the 24th Machine-Gun Company – Sergeant C. B. Popkin and Gunner R. F. Weston – had loosed off a long burst at the triplane as it flew low past them in pursuit of May. A few seconds later, two anti-aircraft Lewis guns of the 53rd Battery, 14th Australian Field Artillery Brigade, manned by Gunners W. J. Evans and R. Buie, had also fired on it. Later, all these men were to claim the responsibility for shooting down von Richthofen.

The triplane's heavy landing was witnessed by Sergeant-Major J. H. Sheridan of the 3rd Battery, Royal Artillery, who had been watching the chase. Sheridan waited for the German pilot to climb out, but when there was no movement the soldier ran forward and peered into the cockpit. The pilot was slumped forward, his head resting against the butt of one of his machine-guns. One hand still gripped the stick. Blood oozed from his mouth and from a hole in his chest where a bullet had made its exit, having entered the right side and traversed his body. There was no doubt that he was dead.

The following day, a British aircraft flew over the German aerodrome at Cappy and dropped a message. It read: 'To the German Flying Corps. Rittmeister Baron Manfred von Richthofen was killed in aerial combat on 21 April 1918. He was buried with full military honours. From the British Royal Air Force.'

Von Richthofen's body was later removed to a German war cemetery, and in 1925 it was finally laid to rest in Berlin. Roy Brown flew several more missions before being sent to hospital in England, suffering from severe stomach trouble and nervous strain. After the war he went back to Canada and became a businessman. He died in 1944. Lieutenant May went on to score thirteen victories and win a DFC. He also returned to Canada, where he made a career in civil aviation. He died in 1952.

Although Roy Brown was officially credited with the killing of von Richthofen, no one really knows to this day whose bullet sent him down. Except to adherents of the 'Red Baron cult' which has grown in recent years along with the upsurge of interest in First World War aviation, the fact of who killed him is relatively unimportant.

What was important was the profound effect his death had on millions of Germans, soldiers and civilians alike. According to General Ludendorff, the psychological impact of his death was equivalent to the loss of thirty divisions. The Richthofen Geschwader continued to fight hard under new commanders – the last of whom was Hermann Goering – but the loss of von Richthofen's personal leadership was noticeable. For the German Air Corps, it was as though that fateful April day in 1918 marked the start of the final slide to defeat.

5 Mick Mannock, VC: the One-Eyed Ace

A few weeks after the death in action of Werner Voss, several pilots of No. 56 Squadron, RFC, learned that they had been awarded decorations. Among them was Rhys-Davids, who had shot Voss down and who received the DSO. That night, No. 56's mess was the scene of a wild party, and Rhys-Davids was reluctantly dragged to his feet to make a speech. In it, he praised the qualities of the German pilots, and asked his colleagues to raise their glasses to the greatest enemy of all: Manfred von Richthofen.

They all rose and drank – all except for one man, a visitor from a neighbouring unit. Setting down his glass, he remained seated. When the others looked at him, he said quietly: 'I won't drink a toast to that bastard.'

Captain Edward Mannock had seen too many of his comrades die, many of them wrapped in agonizing flames, to feel any sense of chivalry about the bitter business of killing.

At the age of thirty, Irish-born Mannock was much older than most fighter pilots. He had two infirmities, one physical, the other psychological. The physical one was a very bad left eye; the psychological one was a chip on his shoulder, the result of a hard struggle for existence during his boyhood and youth. His father had been a corporal in the British Army, and in the late nineteenth century a corporal's pay did not go very far. Day after day, as a child, he had watched his mother struggle to feed himself, his elder brother and elder sister, while others more fortunate squandered money like water. To help out he had been forced to leave school early, working first as a delivery boy for a grocer in Canterbury and then as a barber's assistant. In the end he became a linesman for the Post Office; it was a job he liked, and the family with whom he lodged in Wellingborough gave him much of the affection he had missed as a child. It helped to remove many of the scars of his boyhood and kept him from being too embittered. Nevertheless, 'Mick' Mannock was to remain a confirmed socialist to the end of his days, fondly nurturing a dream that he and others like him would one day be able to change the world.

When he was twenty he had experienced a sudden urge to see the world, working his way through the Middle East and Turkey. It matured him, and the sights he saw led him to believe that Britain might not be such a bad place after all. At any rate, he was not slow to enlist when he believed war to be inevitable in 1914, joining the Medical Corps in the first instance. This, however, was a non-combatant role, and Mannock wanted to fight, so that he applied for a transfer to the Royal Flying Corps, bluffing his way through the medical examinations by memorizing eye-charts.

He was accepted for flying training in 1916, and was fortunate to have as his instructor a man who was already experienced in combat: Captain James McCudden. He taught Mannock all the tricks of his new trade, and the two became firm friends. It was a partnership that only death would sever.

Early in 1917 Mannock joined No. 40 Squadron in France, and it was now that McCudden's teaching paid off. Mannock worked hard to improve his flying and shooting, and despite his bad eye became a better than average marksman. Unlike many of his colleagues, he approached the business of air fighting with extreme caution, preferring to skirt the fringes of his early air skirmishes rather than throw caution to the winds and dive into the middle of the scrap. Some of his fellow pilots even began to hint that he might lack courage, but Mannock took no notice. He watched his more hot-headed critics go down in flames one after the other, and knew that he was right.

After two months, Mannock was satisfied with the tactics he had been striving to perfect, and now his colleagues watched open-mouthed at the change that came over him in action. In the next three weeks he shot down six enemy aircraft, earning the Military Cross and rapid promotion to flight commander. Now that he could impart his skills to other pilots, he really began to come into his own, forging a first-rate fighting team. His pilots had the utmost trust in him; he shepherded them carefully, never lost his head in action, and always ensured that the odds were right before committing himself to battle. He became a master of ambush, and before attacking an enemy he made certain that his pilots conformed to his golden rule: 'Always above, seldom on the same level, never beneath.' He taught his men to attack from astern, if possible, hitting the enemy on the first diving pass. He also taught them the full range of aerobatics to build up their confidence in their aircraft, at the same time stressing that aerobatics in a dogfight were useless and dangerous. Tight turns, he said, were the only manœuvres that paid real dividends in an air battle.

His attitude towards the Germans was simple: he hated them with a deep, implacable loathing that intensified as the months went by. At times, particularly when one of 'his' youngsters failed to return, he was like a man demented; when that happened, killing Germans was his sole obsession. The rage he felt would have made other men foolhardy; in Mannock the effect was exactly the opposite. He became icily efficient, cold-blooded and calculating. And woe betide any German who got into his sights at such a time.

Behind the superb fighting machine he had become lay one overriding fear, and Mannock was not ashamed to admit it. Before each flight he would carefully check his revolver, to make sure that it was loaded and in good working order. If he caught fire in the air, one of those bullets was for himself. Mick Mannock had a horror of burning to death.

He seemed to feel none of this horror, however, when he saw one of his enemies meet with a similar fate. In fact, the sight of a German aircraft and its occupant burning up as it fell seemed to hold a morbid fascination, not to say exultation, for him. 'Sizzle, sizzle – I sent one of the bastards to hell in flames today,' he would shout to his fellow pilots.

Another somewhat macabre fascination was collecting souvenirs from the wrecks of the aircraft he shot down. These he sent off to Jim Eyles, the man with whose family he had lodged in Wellingborough.

'I sent the parcel off to you yesterday [he wrote to Eyles at the beginning of August 1917]. Pilot's boots which belonged to a dead pilot. Goggles belonging to another. The cigarette holder and case were given to me by the captain observer of a two-seater I brought down. The piece of fabric with a number on it is from another Hun two-seater. The other little brown packet is a field dressing carried by a Hun observer for dressing wounds when in the air. I got it from a crashed bus. . . .

'We have only lost six of our original squadron and have brought down about forty-five Huns. My total is now forty-one, although you may not believe it, and they have given me the DSO. I'm expecting the Bar at any moment, as I have brought down another eight since I was recommended for the DSO. If I have any luck, I think I may beat old Mac (McCudden). Then I shall try and oust old Richthofen. . . .'

At the end of the year, by which time he had been transferred to No. 74 Squadron, Mannock's score had risen to fifty-six and he had indeed surpassed 'old Mac'. His reputation as a leader had preceded him, and the young pilots in his charge regarded him with awe and admiration. One of them was Lieutenant Ira 'Taffy' Jones, who many years later was to compile a history of No. 74 Squadron and who described his first meeting with Mannock:

'I arrived at the Squadron late at night, rather shy and frightened. Mannock was in the Mess, and he looked after me just like a big brother. I was posted to his Flight, and he did not allow me to cross the lines for over a week; during this time he took me up twice on a line patrol and we had several practice flights. His advice to me was always to follow my leader, keep my eyes and ears open and keep a silent tongue. It was wonderful to be in his Flight; to him his Flight was everything and he lived for it. Every member had his special thought and care.'

Jones, too, was full of praise for Mannock's prowess in action. On 25 May 1918 he noted in his diary:

'The CO saved Giles's skin today. Giles very carelessly allowed a black Albatros to pounce on him while he was concentrating on the destruction of a silver-grey two-seater. Giles has had his leg pulled unmercifully; we declare he was decoyed. Pilots hate admitting that they have been taken in as a sucker!

'Clements tells me that Mick saved his life tonight, too. Mick and Clements went up for a bit of fun after tea. They each got what they wanted.... Clements spotted a large formation of Huns obviously making a beeline for them. Clements put on full throttle ... to catch up to Mick, who as usual was wasting no time in getting at his enemy. Mick had seen the Hun formation all the time ... he turned west quickly and dived, the Huns following and firing. Mick saved Clements by losing height directly beneath them and so drawing them on to him, while Clements got clear. Clements says it was a rotten sight to see one SE being attacked by such a bunch, and that had it been anyone except Mick, he would have been anxious about his safety. (We all believe that no Hun will ever shoot down Mick.) One Pfalz followed him very closely, and suddenly Mick went down out of control; on his back – spinning – and doing everything imaginable from 8000 to 4000 feet. At 5000 feet the Hun, completely fooled, flattened out to watch the crash. Mick then decided he had had enough, and flattened out too and made for our lines – diving hard.'

And four days later, on the twenty-ninth, Jones wrote:

'Mick took Clements and me up at 7 pm ... Mick spotted about a dozen Huns coming from the direction of Roubaix; we were then over Lille. As we had not too much time for a fight, having already been up for over an hour, he decided to go straight at them, as we had a slight advantage of height. The Huns, who were Albatros Scouts, were of the stout variety, and they accepted our head-on challenge. Both Mick and the

Hun leader opened fire at one another as they approached from about 300 yards' range, but nothing happened. This burst of fire was the signal for a glorious dogfight – as fine and as frightening a dogfight as I've ever been in. Friend and foe fired at and whistled past one another at a tornado pace . . . I have never been so frightened in my life. Of late I have been able to keep very cool during the actual fight, but tonight I became so flustered that occasionally I fired at my own pals in an effort not to miss a chance – thank God, my shooting was erratic. How terrible it would have been if I had, say, shot Mick down! The thought gives me the very creeps . . . Mick sent two slate-blue Albatroses down out of control, and Clements crashed his first Hun. He is very bucked about it. It is wonderful how cheered a pilot becomes after he shoots down his first machine; his morale increases by at least a hundred per cent. This is why Mick gives Huns away – to raise the morale of the beginner.'

This last was a reference to Mannock's habit of allowing new pilots to administer the *coup de grâce* to enemy aircraft already damaged by his own fire, so allowing them to claim the credit. In this he was not alone; many other exceptional air leaders did the same.

Mannock's own combat reports were always extremely brief and to the point. On 1 June 1918, for example, he dismissed the destruction of two, and possibly three, Pfalz in these few terse words:

'Observed and engaged formation of EA scouts east of Merville. Attacked from the front and above. The highest Scout being behind, SE opened fire with both guns at point-blank range. The EA's bottom wings fell off and it crashed. Confirmed also by Lts Giles and Birch.

'Engaged another EA and after a short vertical burst at close range, this Scout burst into flames. Confirmed by all other members of patrol.

'Engaged another EA, which was turning towards me on the same level. Fired several short bursts at this machine whilst circling. This EA went into a spin, and disappeared from the fight.'

Father figure though he may have been to the pilots under his command, Mannock was capable of ruthlessness when it came to enforcing discipline in the air. On patrol, he refused to let any member of his Flight break formation except in the event of engine trouble, and once fired a burst at one young pilot who did so. His single-minded attitude to air fighting almost amounted to mania, particularly when it came to overcoming fear. Mannock himself was often afraid, and was not ashamed to admit it. Real courage, he insisted, lay in a man's ability to overcome fear. One of his favourite sayings, which he was fond of passing on to others, was: 'The will can always triumph over matter during the early stages of a nervous disability, particularly when that disability is only fear.'

Mannock had the utmost sympathy for anyone who admitted he was afraid in the air, yet who went on and did his job in spite of it. To anyone suspected of cowardice, however, he could be merciless. When one of his pilots came to him once and said that he did not have the courage to go into action, Mannock tore off his pilot's wings and made him sew a piece of yellow cloth in their place.

The fact that Mannock took such a step, deliberately humiliating a colleague, was perhaps an indication of his own mental state. He was highly strung at the best of times, and by the summer of 1918 there is little doubt that he was beginning to break under the strain of constant action. He was, to use the parlance of a later generation of pilots, 'twitched'. His hatred of the Germans was now quite pathological; he regarded them as noxious vermin, to be stamped out at all costs. He became prone to bouts of depression, and his mood was reflected in a letter to his sister in June 1918:

'Things are getting a bit intense just lately and I don't quite know how long my nerves will last out. I am rather old now, as airmen go, for fighting. Still, one hopes for the best.... These times are so horrible that occasionally I feel that life is not worth hanging on to myself.... I am supposed to be going on leave on the nineteenth of this month (if I live long enough) and I shall call at Birmingham to see you all.'

Mannock did live long enough to go on leave. On his return to the front in July he was posted to command No. 82 Squadron, and wept unashamedly at leaving his beloved 74 – the squadron he had helped to mould into a fine fighting team, establishing a tradition that would endure down the years.

When Mannock returned to action, his personal score stood at seventy-four enemy aircraft destroyed. It was probably much higher. Later, his achievements would be recognized by the award of the Victoria Cross – but Mick Mannock would never live to wear it.

Towards the end of July, during a dogfight, he hit a German aircraft and followed it down to make sure of a kill – breaking one of his own cardinal rules. He was hit by ground fire, and fell in flames.

6 Albert Ball, VC

Among the names of celebrated Allied pilots to emerge from the bitter fighting over the western front between 1914 and 1918, one in particular stands high in the order of merit: that of Albert Ball. He was the first British pilot to be turned into a national hero as the result of a publicity campaign, just as Immelmann was Germany's first air hero, and as a consequence his name was to become a household word.

Yet – in common with many other pilots who rose to brief fame like meteors over Flanders – Ball's flying career had a very shaky beginning. In the course of his flying training he suffered two bad crashes, and after the second an irate instructor told him that he would never be a pilot – unless he could find a flying school that trained silly girls. But Ball persevered with a determination that was one of his main characteristics, and in due course presented the Royal Flying Corps and the nation with a living legend.

Born in Nottingham, Albert Ball was the son of a well-to-do estate agent. The boy showed a mechanical aptitude at an early age, and in fact became one of the first amateur radio enthusiasts in Britain, picking up and deciphering Morse messages from all over the continent on his primitive wireless. His greatest love, however, was for engines.

He and his younger brother would save their pocket money to buy old engines that were due to be scrapped and spend hours tinkering with them. They usually managed to get them going.

Apart from engines, the other passion in Albert's life was playing the violin. It was his main form of relaxation, and he was very proficient. It brought out another side of his nature; a gentle side which, among other things, made him hate the idea of war and killing.

From his father he inherited a strong business instinct, and on completing his studies he set himself up as an electrical engineer and brass founder. The little business was already beginning to show promise when, in August 1914, Britain and Germany went to war. Ball's belief in the righteousness of Britain's cause outweighed his dislike of fighting, and he immediately volunteered for the Army.

Soon after beginning his training, Ball became attracted to the idea of flying. His unit was stationed near Hendon, where there was a civilian flying school, and he started taking lessons. When his unit moved, he bought himself a motor-cycle and rode the sixty miles to Hendon two or three times a week, setting off at three in the morning and returning in time to be on parade at eight. He eventually qualified for his pilot's certificate on a Caudron biplane in October 1915 – and at once applied for a transfer to the Royal Flying Corps.

At Upavon, the Central Flying School, Ball soon found that the RFC's brand of flying was much more rigorous and exacting than anything he had encountered so far. Despite his early lack of expertise, however, he attained the required standard of proficiency, and early in 1916 he left for France to join No. 13 Squadron. He was just nineteen years old.

His squadron, flying BE2c biplanes, was engaged on

army co-operation duties, which involved photographing German trench patterns, artillery spotting, reconnaissance and, occasionally, dropping light bombs and grenades. Ball arrived in France at a time when the RFC's observation aircraft were suffering heavy losses from the enemy anti-aircraft fire, which was becoming more concentrated and accurate, and particularly from the Fokker monoplanes which ranged over the front. The young pilots threw themselves into the inferno twice, sometimes three times a day, and their life expectancy was measured in weeks. Many of those who survived were wrecks, their nerves shattered, trembling old men at the age of nineteen or twenty.

Under these hazardous conditions Ball soon began to win a reputation as a dare-devil. He seemed always to be on the look-out for trouble, often going out of his way to attack enemy aircraft. There is no doubt that he enjoyed more than his fair share of luck, but nevertheless in these early days he learned many lessons which were to prove invaluable during his later career as a fighter pilot. Foremost among them was the vital importance of keeping a good look-out; he failed to do so on one occasion when he was attacking a lone Albatros two-seater, and almost met his end when the Fokkers he had failed to see lurking above pounced on him.

Ball's aggressive tactics certainly seemed to pay dividends. During his first two months at the front he enabled his observer to shoot down three enemy aircraft by carefully manœuvring his BE into the right position. His one desire, however, was to fly single-seaters, and as often as possible he took up 13 Squadron's solitary Bristol Scout to practise his shooting with the little machine's single Lewis gun. Finally, in May 1916, he succeeded in being transferred to No. 11 Squadron, which was re-equipping with Nieuport Scouts.

Ball was completely at home in the highly manœuvr-able Nieuport. Since his squadron did not yet possess enough aircraft of this type to make team fighting possible, he usually patrolled alone, and was to remain a solitary fighter for most of his career. He shot down his first two enemy aircraft at the end of May and began to distinguish himself in the horrific Somme battle that unfolded a few weeks later. On 22 August, for example, he destroyed three enemy machines in one day, and repeated the per-formance a week later. He was now flying with No. 60 Squadron, and in September 1916 this unit carried out many attacks on enemy kite balloons. On one occasion, Ball and another pilot named Lieutenant Walters set out to attack some balloons with Le Prieur rockets, only to find that the balloons had been hauled down. Flying on, the two British airmen sighted a pair of German machines, a Roland and an LVG, Ball fired his rockets at the Roland and missed, but shot the German down with his Lewis gun. Walters, however, saw his rocket salvo strike the LVG and explode, tearing the enemy aircraft to pieces. It was probably the first time in history that an aircraft was destroyed by air-to-air rockets.

During this period, Ball perfected the tactics he was to employ in most of his subsequent air fights. They were revolutionary for their time, and to most of his con-temporaries they seemed hair-raising. They certainly re-quired excellent judgement and split-second timing. He would, for example, deliberately allow an enemy aircraft to get on his tail and then, just as the other was about to open fire – a moment Ball could gauge with uncanny skill – he would whip round in a tight turn and come up on the German's tail. Another technique was to attack the enemy head on, sticking grimly to his course and banking on the German losing his nerve. It always worked; the enemy pilot would break sharply away just as a collision seemed inevitable, and in that fraction of a second Ball would put a burst into him.

In the Autumn of 1916 Ball, together with several other seasoned air fighters, was transferred to a training unit to pass on his skills to fresh pilots. He found the routine of instructing exceedingly dull, and was never very good at it; he was too much of an individualist for things to be otherwise. He badgered his superiors for a posting back to the front, and made an attempt to explain the burning desire he felt to get back into the fighting in a revealing letter to his mother:

'I have offered, dear, to go out again and have another smack. I don't offer because I want to go, but because every boy who has loving people and a good home should go out and stand up for it. You think I have done enough, but oh, no, there is not, or at least should not be, such a thought in such a war as this. . . . It is an honour to be able to fight and do one's best for such a country as this and for such dear people. I shall fight for you and come home for you, and God always looks after me and makes me strong; may He look after you also.

'I only scrap because it is my duty, and I do not think anything bad about the Hun. He is just a good chap with very little guts, trying to do his best. Nothing makes me feel more rotten than to see them go down; but, you see, it is either them or me, so I must do my best to make it a case of *them*. I am, indeed, looked after by God; but oh, I do get tired of always living to kill. I am beginning to feel like a murderer. I shall be pleased when I have finished. Oh, won't it be nice when all this beastly killing is over, and we can just enjoy ourselves and not hurt anyone? I hate this game, but it is the only thing one must do just now.'

It was a 'game' at which he excelled, despite his school-boyish concept of war and his deeply religious sentiments – sentiments that probably never took into account the fact that the men he was killing wore a belt whose buckle bore the inscription 'God with us'.

Ball got his way at last, and towards the end of February 1917 he was posted to No. 56 Squadron as a Flight Commander. This squadron was equipped with the latest British fighter, the SE5, which had a top speed of 120 mph and could climb to 18,000 feet. It was armed with two machine-guns, one firing through the propeller and the other mounted on top of the wing. Although Ball always said that he preferred the Nieuport, there was no doubt that the SE5 was one of the best combat aircraft to be produced in the war.

Ball found his new task far from easy. He was used to solitary work, and now he found himself responsible for a flight of six aircraft whose pilots depended on his leadership for their survival. Yet, in between the routine patrols, which took place usually twice a day, he found time for lone excursions. They almost invariably ended in a fight, with Ball often tackling vastly superior odds.

One day, while patrolling well inside enemy territory, Ball spotted two enemy aircraft and dived to attack them, firing at them without causing serious damage until he finally ran out of ammunition. At that moment the Germans turned and ran for home. Ball followed them blazing away at them with his only remaining weapon – his service revolver. He saw them land, then circled at a safe distance while he scribbled a hasty note. Swooping down, he dropped the weighted scrap of paper on the enemy field; it challenged the same two enemy pilots to a duel at the same time the next day.

He arrived back over the enemy field on schedule, and to his delight he saw the two German machines making wide circles overhead. He at once dived to the attack – and suddenly realized that he had fallen into a trap. Once again he had forgotten to check the dangerous sector of sky behind his tail, and now, glancing round, he saw three more enemy machines diving at him. Running for home was out of the question, for the enemy aircraft were cutting off his line of retreat. There was no alternative but to accept combat.

For the next few minutes the six machines twisted and turned, the lone Englishman looking out all the time for some way of escape and firing at his adversaries in short bursts whenever the opportunity arose. Then, to his horror, he ran out of ammunition. It was only a question of time before he was cornered and sent down in flames.

Suddenly, he had a brilliant idea. Spotting a large field below, he throttled back and glided down to land. As he rolled to a stop, he slumped in the cockpit as though he had been hit. Out of the corner of his eye, he saw the five German machines roar low overhead. Three flew away in the direction of their airfield, presumably to spread the good news that the great Albert Ball had been shot down; the other two came in to land, their pilots obviously intent on taking Ball prisoner if he still lived.

Ball, very much alive, had kept his engine idling the whole time. He saw the German pilots climb from their cockpits and come running towards him – and at that moment he gunned his engine and sent the SE lurching forward over the uneven ground. As he lifted into the air and turned, he saw the two Germans running frantically back to their aircraft – but they were too late. By the time they got airborne again, Ball was well on his way back to the lines.

It was typical of the man, and his coolness in even the most impossible situation. On another occasion, he sighted five enemy aircraft and immediately attacked them despite the weight of the odds against him. Within two minutes he destroyed two of the enemy machines, and then, as the other three came at him from different directions and their bullets smacked through his SE's wings and fuselage, he deliberately put his aircraft into a spin. One of the Germans followed him down in a steep dive, but the enemy pilot was not as quick to recover as Ball. As the Englishman pulled out with only feet to spare, the German behind him flew into the ground. The two remaining Huns now dived to the attack, and Ball pulled up to meet them in a climbing turn. One of the aircraft crossed his sights and he fired, his bullets tearing a wing off the enemy machine. The sole survivor left the scene as fast as possible.

Brilliant though his tactics were, they did not always work out exactly as he had planned. One day early in 1917, for example, he sighted two Albatros Scouts and attacked them, quickly sending one of them down out of control. He then turned on the other, hurtling at it head-on. The two fighters streaked towards one another at a closing speed of over 200 mph. Ball knew that his fire was hitting the enemy machine, for he could see his tracers disappearing into it. But still it came on, and now it was so close that Ball could distinguish the pilot's goggled face. At that instant, Ball's aircraft shuddered and oil spurted into his face as bullets smacked into his engine. Temporarily blinded, he tensed himself and waited for the shattering impact. He waited for a second that seemed like an eternity – and nothing happened. Wiping the oil from his eyes, he looked round. There was no sign of the German aircraft. Then he saw it: a shattered wreck on the ground. The enemy pilot, hit by Ball's bullets, must have slumped over the stick at the very last instant, sending his machine into its last dive. Ball knew that he had missed being rammed by a matter of inches.

Ball was so eager to get to grips with the enemy that he practically lived in a tent next to his aircraft, ready to jump into the cockpit at a moment's notice. On several occasions, roused from his bed by the news of enemy aircraft crossing the lines, he went into action still wearing his pyjamas. He hardly ever wore a flying helmet, and the somewhat romantic story did the rounds of the English newspapers (originated by a journalist who had never actually met Ball) that it was because he liked to feel the wind in his hair. The truth was much more mundane: a flying helmet chafed the back of Ball's neck, and he felt that it restricted his head movements when searching the sky behind. One story the Press fortunately never got hold of was that Ball's squadron colleagues, although they had the utmost respect for him, thought him rather weird at times. After all, what else were they to think about a man who lit a red flare outside his tent and walked round and round it in the middle of the night, playing a violin?

Early in 1917 Ball's score was running neck-and-neck with that of the French ace Georges Guynemer, and the newspapers were not slow to seize on the friendly rivalry that was growing between the two. At the beginning of May Ball passed Guynemer's total, and now there was much speculation as to whether he would catch up with von Richthofen, who at that time had fifty-two kills to his credit.

Ball and No. 56 Squadron had skirmished with von Richthofen's *Jagdstaffel* 11 on several occasions, but Ball had never made contact with the Red Baron himself. In May 1917, the British learned that von Richthofen had gone home on leave and his unit had been taken over in his absence by his brother, Lothar; with the Baron off the scene, it seemed a good opportunity to bring *Jagdstaffel* 11 to combat and inflict some losses on it.

In the evening of 7 May, therefore, two RFC squadrons –

one of them No. 56 – set out to mount an offensive patrol over *Jagdstaffel* 11's airfield at Douai. One of 56's pilots, Cecil Lewis, described the scene:

'The May evening is heavy with threatening masses of cumulus cloud, majestic skyscapes, solid-looking as snow mountains, fraught with caves and valleys, rifts and ravines.... Steadily the body of scouts rises higher and higher, threading its way between the cloud precipices. Sometimes, below, the streets of a village, the corner of a wood, a few dark figures moving, glides into view like a slide into a lantern and is then hidden again....

'A red light curls up from the leader's cockpit and falls away. Action! He alters direction slightly, and the patrol, shifting throttle and rudder, keep close like a pack of hounds on the scent. He has seen, and they see soon, six scouts three thousand feet below. Black crosses! It seems interminable till the eleven come within diving distance. The pilots nurse their engines, hard-minded and set, test their guns and watch their indicators. At last the leader sways sideways, as a signal that each should take his man, and suddenly drops....'

As the fight was joined it suddenly began to rain, cutting down the visibility. Desperately, the section leaders of No. 56 Squadron tried to hold their men together, but in the confusion of the dogfight the squadron became badly dislocated. Some of the SE5s ran for home, others headed for a pre-arranged rendezvous over Arras. There, Albert Ball joined up with another Flight Commander named Crowe and the two continued patrol, joined by a lone Spad. Near Loos, Ball suddenly fired a couple of Very lights and dived on a red-and-yellow Fokker triplane, following it into a cloud.

It was the last time that Ball was seen alive. Of the

eleven SE5s that had set out, in fact, only five returned to base, and No. 56 Squadron's mess was very subdued that night. Then someone took his place at the piano, the singing started and the drink began to flow. Such was the custom of the RFC; the dead were dead, and there was another day tomorrow. Later in the evening someone asked Cecil Lewis, who had a fine tenor voice, if he would sing. He rose to his feet, and in the silence the words of Stevenson's 'Requiem' rang out through the room:

> Under the wide and starry sky,
> Dig the grave and let me lie.
> Glad did I live and gladly die,
> And I laid me down with a will.
>
> These be the words you grave for me:
> Here he lies where he longed to be;
> Home is the sailor, home from the sea,
> And the hunter home from the hill.

They all knew it was a kind of epitaph for Ball, and many eyes held tears as the notes died away. Then someone began to sing 'Pack up your troubles', and in a flash the mood changed as the drink and the noise took effect. They had already begun to forget.

On the German airfield at Douai, the Germans were celebrating too. Not only had Lothar von Richthofen returned safely to base in an aircraft shot full of holes, but he claimed that he had shot down Albert Ball. Although he believed his claim to be justified – he had, in fact, hit Ball's aircraft several times – it later transpired that the British ace had been shot down by a machine-gun mounted on a church steeple. The Germans buried him near Lille, and dropped a message to that effect over No. 56's aerodrome.

A month later, it was announced that Captain Albert

Ball, DSO, MC, had been posthumously awarded the Victoria Cross. His score of enemy aircraft destroyed at the time of his death was forty-three. Other pilots were to achieve higher figures; but none would inspire such determination among those who followed as the twenty-year-old from Nottingham who hated war, and yet who fought with matchless courage.

7 Major McCudden, VC

High above the fields of northern France, the young pilot banked his DH2 scout first to the right, then to the left, carefully scanning the sky around him. Then, satisfied that he was alone, he took a deep breath and tried to remember everything his instructors had told him just a few weeks earlier. Nose down and throttle open to gain speed, then stick hard back into the stomach.

It was November 1916, and for the first time in his life twenty-one-year-old James McCudden was going to try his hand at a loop.

He pulled back on the stick and the horizon dropped away underneath his nose. All he had to do now was to keep the stick right back and drive the little biplane over the top. It should have been simple – but at the last moment, McCudden panicked. With the aircraft almost vertical, he suddenly changed his mind and shoved the stick forward. The result was dramatic. As the biplane's nose dropped sickeningly, the negative 'g' caused McCudden – and everything else – to become momentarily weightless. Some ammunition drums rose from the floor of the cockpit and shot past the startled pilot's head, striking the 'pusher' propeller behind him with a hideous splintering sound and tearing off three of its four blades.

There was a fearful racket and the whole aircraft began

to judder and vibrate, threatening to shake itself apart. Instinctively, McCudden switched off the engine and brought the DH gingerly out of its dive. Looking back to see what damage had been done, he was horrified to see that one of the aircraft's tail-boom struts had broken clean in half. The next few minutes were the longest of McCudden's life as he cautiously eased his crippled machine down towards a forced landing. He had learned a lesson that day, and it was this: never change your mind once you have committed yourself. It was a lesson he was to apply religiously to his combat flying over the next eighteen months; once the decision had been made, McCudden would stick to it to the bitter end. It was a policy that was to help him become one of the greatest fighter pilots of all time.

James Byford McCudden was born in Gillingham, Kent, in March 1895. His father, an Irishman, was a warrant officer in the Royal Engineers, and after only a basic education James also joined the regiment as a bugler at the age of fourteen. Later, his talent for tinkering with engines led him into the trade of mechanic, and in May 1913 he transferred to the Royal Flying Corps, which was then only a year old.

In August 1914 he went to France with No. 3 Squadron, the first RFC unit to be sent to the continent following the outbreak of war. A few months later he succeeded in transferring to aircrew, becoming an observer on BE2cs. By the time he was promoted to Flight Sergeant in 1916 he had already destroyed two enemy aircraft, displaying an accuracy that astonished his pilots.

His superiors, recognizing that the young man had considerable potential as an air fighter and that his experience with the RFC more than adequately made up for his lack of background and educational qualifications, sent him back to England to train as a pilot. On gaining his wings he was posted to No. 29 Squadron, flying DH2s, and on 6 September he scored his first victory as pilot when he shot down an AEG two-seater between Ypres and Armentieres. As soon as he saw McCudden approaching, the German pilot dived away towards his own lines and McCudden only just managed to stay with him, firing two drums of ammunition from extreme range before the AEG finally went down. After this encounter McCudden practised long-range shooting at every opportunity and it eventually became his speciality.

On 17 January 1917 he had a narrow escape when he was shot down by a Fokker DII. He escaped unhurt from the crash-landing, but it was a sobering experience. For the first time, he realized that air fighting was a science rather than a hit-or-miss business, and from now on he began to make a careful study of German tactics. Later, he was to be acknowledged as one of the RFC's greatest tactical experts.

A couple of weeks after his crash, McCudden was sent to England as an instructor for a short time, and it was during this period that he met and befriended Mick Mannock. The two men had a great deal in common, although 'Old Mac' could never share Mannock's bitter hatred of the Germans.

McCudden was still in England in the spring and early summer of 1917, the period that saw some of the most bitter air fighting of the entire war. He was itching to get back into action, and when formations of twin-engined Gotha bombers began to raid London and towns on the south-east coast he asked for permission to have a go at them. His chance came one day in June, when he learned that a Gotha formation was crossing the coast just as he himself had landed at Croydon. Hastily taking off again, he flew back to his own airfield in Kent, where he had a machine-gun fitted to the mounting on the upper wing of his Sopwith Pup. Grabbing a few drums of ammunition, he took off and climbed hard through the clouds, eventually sighting the Gothas heading homewards at 15,000 feet. He chased the enemy formation out over the North Sea, loosing off several bursts at long range, but he could not catch up with the bombers and they got away.

This was the first big daylight raid on London, and although no fewer than ninety-two British aircraft took off to intercept the Gothas the bombers all returned safely to their bases. McCudden, furious at his personal failure to intercept the bombers, realized that the air war had progressed a long way in the few short months since he had left the front, and the realization made him more determined than ever to get back into combat.

He returned to France in July, to fly Sopwith Pups with No. 66 Squadron. His stay on this occasion was to be limited, for his assignment was in the nature of a refresher course designed to bring him up to date with the latest techniques in air fighting. No. 66 was one of four squadrons occupying an airfield at Estree Blanche, opposite the sector of the front patrolled by von Richthofen's *Jagdgeschwader*. McCudden found that the day of the lone patrol was over, although it was still practised by one or two individualists, and that teamwork was now the vital aspect of air combat.

McCudden was particularly interested in the operational record of No. 56 Squadron, whose pilots had brought the matter of teamwork to a fine art. The unit was equipped with SE5s; McCudden borrowed one and shot down an Albatros, and from that moment he never flew any other type of aircraft in combat. The SE, as far as he was concerned – although perhaps not as manœuvrable as other types he had flown – was the best fighter ever designed.

In August 1917 McCudden was posted to No. 56

Squadron as a Flight Commander. At that time he had seven enemy aircraft to his credit, but he was still very much an unknown quantity to many of the squadron's pilots and they waited with interest to see how he would shape up as a fighting leader. They soon found out: in three days he shot down three more enemy machines. From then on his score mounted steadily, and the more he engaged in combat the more his admiration grew for the new generation of German pilots – among them Werner Voss, who fell in the course of that gallant last fight with McCudden and his men in September already described.

During the winter of 1917 there were fewer air battles between large fighter formations, mainly because the weather was unsuitable for large-scale offensive patrols. The emphasis now switched to intercepting and destroying the enemy's two-seater observation aircraft, which slipped over the lines at heights of anything up to 20,000 feet. By stripping down his aircraft and making sure that his engine was in first-class condition McCudden found that he could climb to this height for limited periods, and shooting down reconnaissance machines became a speciality. It was not an easy task, for the enemy machines were often heavily armoured and, in the hands of an experienced pilot, they could usually hold their own against a single-seat fighter. Nevertheless, McCudden found that the secret lay first of all in putting the German gunner out of action, preferably in a surprise attack that involved coming up from below in the enemy's blind spot and following every manœuvre made by the two-seater until the fighter was close enough to open fire.

It was not often, however, that a fighter emerged from a combat with a two-seater without having suffered some kind of battle damage, and McCudden was no exception, as one of his combat reports tells:

'Got to lines at Masnieres at 10.10 and patrolled from Gouzeaucourt to Bourlon. Clouds at 2000 feet. At 10.45 drove several EA Scouts away from Bourlon. EAA very active and accurate. At 11.15 saw 2 EA two-seaters coming west over Fontaine. I secured a good position behind front EA and fired a good burst from both guns. EA's engine stopped and water streamed from radiator. As EA glided west, I let him land OK and then landed myself, as EA gunner had hit my radiator with explosive bullet. EA landed south-east of Havrincourt intact with exception of bullet holes. The pilot badly wounded. . . .'

What McCudden omitted to mention about this action, which occurred on 30 November 1917, was that he personally placed the enemy machine under guard and cared for the injured German as best he could until some British troops arrived on the scene.

Three days later, McCudden received a brand-new SE5a; its serial number was A4891, and he was to fly this machine for the remainder of his time with 56 Squadron. Over the propeller boss, McCudden fitted a red spinner which he had taken from a shot-down LVG; it fitted perfectly and the extra streamlining added several miles an hour to the aircraft's top speed. Apart from the spinner, McCudden's aircraft was easily distinguished by the large number '6' painted in white on the upper surface and in black on the lower surface of the wings.

While flying this machine, McCudden scored a series of notable victories in December. On the twenty-second he shot down a DFW from such close range that the observer's blood spattered his SE, and the next day he destroyed four two-seaters between first light and dusk. During his first patrol of the day he skirmished with three enemy aircraft, but this fight was inconclusive. Then he spotted an LVG on its way home from a reconnaissance of the lines, and after a brief action shot it down near La Frère. Soon afterwards he destroyed a second two-seater near Peronne. In the course of a second patrol that afternoon he shot down a second LVG and a Rumpler.

He repeated this exploit five days later, on the twenty-eighth, and his combat report tells the story:

'Left aerodrome at 10.15 to look for EA west of the lines. At 11.10 I saw a Rumpler coming west over Boursies. I got into position at seventy-five yards, fired a short burst from both guns, when EA at once went into a right-hand spiral dive and its right-hand wings fell off at about 17,000, and the wreckage fell in our lines north of Velu Wood at 11.15. At 11.30 saw a Rumpler going north over Havrincourt at 17,000. I secured a firing position and fired a good burst from both guns, when flames at once came from EA's fuselage and he went down in a right-hand flat spin and crashed in our lines near Flers (as near as I could judge as I remained at 17,000 feet so as not to lose time by going down and having to climb up again). EA crashed about 11.35 am.

'I now saw an LVG being shelled by our AA over Havrincourt at 16,000. AA fire did not stop until I was within range of EA. I obtained a good position at fairly long range, fired a burst with the object of making him dive, which he did. EA dived very steeply (about 200 mph), starting at about 16,000 feet, and at about 9000 feet I fired another burst into EA at 100 yards range, when flames issued from EA's fuselage and then he broke up over Havrincourt Wood, the wreckage falling in our lines. The EA had been diving so fast that the hostile observer could not fire even if I gave him the chance [the observer had to stand up to shoot, and at this speed the slipstream would have flattened him against the fuselage].

'I climbed again and at 12.15 at 18,000 I saw an LVG being shelled by our AA over Lagnicourt. EA dived down east and I caught up with him just east of the lines, and fired a good burst from Lewis at 100 yards, when a small burst of flame came from EA but at once went out again. EA dived steeply kicking his rudder from side to side and I last saw him gliding NE over Harquion at 12.20 at 9000 feet, under control. Returned at 12.25 as I had no more petrol.'

It all sounded very simple, the way McCudden described it. But there is nothing simple about spending the best part of two hours in an open cockpit, three miles above the earth, in the middle of winter, and McCudden often returned from these high-level patrols physically sick and exhausted – yet always prepared to fly another one just a few hours later.

During McCudden's time with No. 56 Squadron, the pilots of his flight claimed the destruction of seventy German aircraft for the loss of only four of their own number. It was a fine testimony to 'Old Mac's' power of leadership; his young pilots revered him and would have followed him anywhere. During his time as an instructor, moreover, McCudden trained many pilots who would bear the brunt of the air fighting in 1918; at one time, practically the whole of No. 43 Squadron was composed of fighter pilots who had passed through his capable hands.

In February 1918 McCudden was sent back to England again. He now had a total of fifty-seven enemy aircraft to his credit, and had collected an impressive number of decorations: the Military Medal; Distinguished Service Order and Bar; Military Cross and Bar. 'Consistent gallantry, courage and dash' and 'conspicuous gallantry' were terms that appeared frequently in his citations. Yet he was always modest, and to some degree self-effacing; when his fellow officers dined him out on the night before his return to England, he expressed astonishment at the number of visitors who had come to see him off. He had genuinely never dreamed that he was so popular, or that so many people held him in such high esteem.

Just before his departure, McCudden made one last war flight. He caught a Hanoveraner two-seater over the front line and attacked it savagely, his bullets ripping great chunks from the fuselage. The observer fell from the shattered machine and tumbled to his death like a broken doll; the pilot fought a losing battle to retain control and crashed just inside the German lines. It was No. 56 Squadron's 250th victory.

Soon after his return to England, McCudden was awarded the Victoria Cross. The citation read: 'This officer is considered by the record he has made, by his fearlessness and by the great service he has rendered to his country, deserving of the very highest honour....'

After four months in England, McCudden was promoted Major and ordered back to France to take command of No. 60 Squadron. On 9 July 1918 he crossed the Channel in his SE5 and landed at a French aerodrome to refuel before continuing to No. 60's base.

He took off again a few minutes later, but as he was climbing away his engine suddenly died. Observers on the ground saw the nose of his machine go down as McCudden looked ahead for somewhere to land. One of the cardinal rules of flying is that you never turn back towards the field if your engine fails on take-off; too much height and airspeed are lost in a turn. It was a rule that McCudden had drilled into his pupils during his months as an instructor.

But, incredibly, McCudden started to turn back. Witnesses saw his machine bank, then it stalled and fell, starting to go into a spin. There was not sufficient height to recover. A few seconds later, Major James McCudden lay dead in the splintered wreckage. For the second time in his flying career, he had changed his mind at a crucial moment. This time, the sky had not forgiven his error.

8 Barker's
Last Battle

It was one of those magic mornings when the war seemed a million miles away. High above the frost-rimed fields of northern France, Major W. G. Barker felt a profound sense of peace as he watched the clear sunlight glitter on the struts and bracing wires of his little Sopwith Snipe biplane, his senses lulled by the drone of the engine.

It was 27 October 1918, and Bill Barker was leaving the war-torn skies of the western front for good. Just a few minutes earlier, he had said goodbye to his fellow pilots of No. 201 Squadron, RAF, and performed a meticulous slow roll over La Targette aerodrome before setting course westwards towards the English Channel. The nightmare-torn sleep, the cold clutch of fear as one sighted the Fokkers sweeping over the horizon in their deadly fan-shaped formations, the horror of seeing one's comrades spinning to the earth engulfed in flames, unable to save themselves because they had no parachutes – all that was behind him now. Ahead lay a few days' leave, and afterwards a posting as CO of a flying school at Hounslow, Middlesex.

The carnage of the western front was a far cry from the broad prairies of Barker's native Canada. Joining the Army on the outbreak of war, he had arrived in France in 1915 with the Canadian Mounted Rifles and spent his twenty-first birthday shivering in the mud of Flanders.

One day, wistfully observing two silvery aircraft tangling in combat far above, he decided that he had had enough; within twenty-four hours he had applied for a transfer to the Royal Flying Corps.

He was accepted as an air gunner and was posted to No. 9 Squadron RFC at Allonville with the lowly rank of Air Mechanic – the equivalent of an army private. At this time, during the closing months of 1915, the RFC was having a hard time at the hands of the deadly Fokker monoplanes, with their forward-firing machine-guns, and Barker's squadron – equipped with slow, ageing BE2c biplanes – was no exception. Survival usually meant the ability to shoot straight and hit the enemy first time, and Barker – who had hunted elk from horseback as a boy – soon proved his worth in that respect. One morning, his aircraft was attacked by a Fokker behind the German lines; Barker swung round his Lewis gun, aimed and fired a burst all in one swift movement. The enemy immediately plummeted down, leaving a trail of smoke and debris.

Soon after this, Barker was granted a commission and posted to No. 4 Squadron as an observer in the early part of 1916. Life during the months that followed was hectic enough; Barker's new squadron was among those taking part in the tragic Battle of the Somme that summer, and he himself was slightly wounded in a brush with an enemy fighter. Barker, however, was not content to fight his war from the rear cockpit, and in the autumn of 1916 he applied for pilot training. The following January he was awarded his coveted wings, and a couple of weeks later he was back in France as a newly-promoted Captain, flying on artillery spotting duties with No. 15 Squadron. During these operations he was slightly wounded again by a shell splinter that sliced open his cheek, bouncing off the cheekbone and narrowly missing his eye. He was flying again the next day.

In the summer of 1917, Barker was given command of No. 28 Squadron, equipped with Sopwith Camels. Barker was delighted with the manoeuvrability of the aircraft, and with the hitting power of its twin Vickers machine-guns – but he was soon made aware that the machine had other points which were by no means as favourable. During the Flanders offensive of 1917, he was attacking enemy troop concentrations on the Ypres–Menin road when his flight was 'bounced' by ten Albatros D5 fighters. A whirling dog-fight ensued, during which Barker lost contact with the rest of his aircraft. Breaking off the combat, he climbed to ten thousand feet and set course for home, entering a layer of cloud.

Suddenly, the controls went haywire as the Camel flicked into a vicious spin. Instinctively, Barker closed the throttle and fought to resume level flight. The altimeter unwound with frightening speed, counting off the thousands of feet. The little fighter tumbled out of the cloud base and Barker saw the earth gyrating around him. None of his corrective actions had worked, and he had almost given himself up for lost when, miraculously, the spinning stopped. Sweating, Barker eased back the stick and the Camel came out of its headlong plunge only 500 feet above the ground.

In the autumn, No. 28 Squadron was sent to the southern front as part of the Allied effort to bolster the Italians, who had suffered a series of reverses in their campaign against the Austrians. At this time Barker's score of enemy aircraft destroyed stood at five, and now, on the Austrian front, the tally began to mount steadily. Right from the start, No. 28 carried the war into the enemy's camp with a series of determined attacks on Austrian airfields. One of the most spectacular of these raids occurred on Christmas Day 1917, when Barker and two other pilots went hunting observation balloons. Barker sent one down in flames over the front line and then headed deep into enemy territory, determined to use up the rest of his incendiary bullets on a worthwhile target.

Locating an Austrian airfield, Barker took his aircraft down to zero feet and roared over the snow-covered terrain at full throttle, selecting the canvas hangars as his target. His first burst must have ripped into the fuel tanks of the aircraft inside, for the hangar exploded in a gout of flame. For the next few minutes he and the other pilots roved back and forth over the aerodrome, shooting up the installations with deadly accuracy. When they finally droned away, they left all the hangars and their contents in flames. On the way home, they exhausted their ammunition on Austrian troops, huddled in their front-line trenches.

Soon after this exploit Barker carried out another successful low-level mission, this time against the Austrian Army Headquarters at San Vito. With five other Camels – each one carrying four small bombs – Barker headed out over the Adriatic, flying low over the sea and parallel to the coast to escape detection. The surprise was complete. Turning inland, the six aircraft swept down on San Vito and sped towards the target – a large, isolated building on the outskirts of the town – in line astern. Each pilot in turn raked the HQ's windows with machine-gun fire, then pulled up sharply and turned to make his bomb-run. Despite heavy small-arms fire, the Camels hit the target several times and returned to base without loss.

During the winter of 1917–18, flying in open cockpits at high altitude over the treacherous mountain regions of north-east Italy became a nightmare, and several pilots were lost when their engines froze and they crashed into the mountain sides. Barker himself survived a serious crash-landing on the lower slopes after his aircraft was hit by machine-gun fire from an Austrian outpost. On another occasion, after sustaining severe battle damage in the course of a dogfight with Austrian aircraft, he crash-landed in the icy waters of Lake Garda. He swam for several minutes, numb with cold, before a rowing-boat picked him up.

Air combats intensified during the spring and early summer of 1918, and there was a particularly hectic period of fighting when the Austrians launched a major offensive in June. In one air battle during this phase, Barker shot down one of Austria's leading air aces, Major Linke, within sight of the latter's own airfield.

Barker went to great lengths to maintain 28 Squadron's offensive spirit. In July 1918 he dropped hundreds of leaflets over the principal Austrian fighter airfields, stating that his squadron would attack them every morning for a fortnight and challenging the Austrian pilots to combat. During that fortnight, he added five enemy aircraft to his score.

Then, in September 1918, Barker was posted back to the western front to command No. 201 Squadron, which was equipped with the latest Sopwith Snipe fighters – a development of the Camel that could climb to 24,000 feet, higher than the newest enemy combat aircraft. Barker's task was to test the Snipe in action, and to perfect new combat techniques. By this time, his confirmed score of aircraft destroyed stood at forty-six. His decorations included the DSO and Bar, MC and two Bars, the *Croix de Guerre* and the Italian Cross of Valour. He was just twenty-four years old.

His time with 201 Squadron was short-lived. For some time, his superiors had been thinking about grounding him before his luck finally ran out; in the end, they decided to give him a safe posting in England.

So it was, on the morning of 27 October 1918, that Bill Barker found himself flying towards the English Channel *en route* for Hounslow. Despite the strain of combat, he was not happy at leaving the front. One thought consoled him; his superiors had promised that he was eventually to be given command of a new Snipe squadron which was then forming in England.

Barker, however, was destined never to arrive at Hounslow. As he cruised high over the Forest of Mormal, something suddenly caught his attention; a momentary flicker in the sky, several thousand feet higher up. It was the wing of a turning aircraft, glittering in the sun, and Barker knew that in this area the chances were that it was a Hun. Immediately, he opened the throttle and eased back the stick, putting the Snipe into a shallow climb.

Carrying out their reconnaissance at twenty thousand feet, the pilot and observer of the German Hanoveraner two-seater were not unduly concerned. At that height, they considered themselves immune from attack. Nevertheless, the enemy observer was wide awake, and he opened fire as Barker came within range, sending Spandau bullets through the fabric of the Canadian's wings.

Barker pressed home his attack, seeing his bullets strike home, but the Hanoveraner flew steadily on. Twice more the Canadian closed in, exchanging bursts of fire with the enemy gunner. Both aircraft were hit repeatedly. Suddenly, Barker decided to change his tactics. Long ago, he had removed the conventional radial sight from his twin Vickers machine-guns and replaced it with a simple peep sight which, he had always claimed, enabled him to place his bursts of fire with greater accuracy. He now used it to good effect, aiming at the German gunner who was still hammering away at him. To his satisfaction, he saw the man throw up his arms and collapse in his cockpit.

The rest was easy. At point-blank range, Barker poured round after round into the now defenceless two-seater. The Hanoveraner seemed to stagger in mid-air and began to break up. Its wings tore off and the fuselage, spinning wildly, plummeted down towards the forest far below. It was Barker's forty-seventh victory.

The Canadian's elation, however, was short-lived. In the heat of the action, he had forgotten one of the most vital and basic rules of air fighting: keep looking behind. It's the one you don't see who gets you!

He never saw the deadly Fokker triplane arcing down on his tail until the German opened fire. Barker knew a confused sensation of whiplash cracks as bullets spattered the Snipe, followed by a spasm of excruciating pain as one of them tore into his right thigh. The Snipe shuddered into an incipient spin which Barker corrected by instinct, half dazed with the shock of his wound. Looking round, he saw the Fokker closing in for the kill and flung his aircraft into a steep turn. The German overshot and Barker pressed the trigger as the enemy flashed past his nose.

It was now that the Canadian's superb marksmanship paid off. The Fokker instantly became a ball of fire, rolling earthwards. Forty-eight!

There was no time for self-congratulation. Pressing his bullet-torn thigh against the side of the cockpit in an effort to ease the fearful pain and stop some of the bleeding, Barker turned the Snipe's nose towards La Targette, hoping to land before he passed out.

Suddenly the sky was full of enemy aircraft, buzzing like wasps on a windowpane. Out of long habit, Barker tried to count them. He reached fifty and wearily gave up. So this was where the road was going to end – the long road that had led him from the prairies of his native Manitoba.

Grimly, convinced that he was going to die, Barker resolved to try and take one or two of his enemies with him. For a fraction of a second a brightly-painted Fokker D7 was spreadeagled in his sights; he fired and the enemy pilot slumped over the controls, the aircraft coming apart as it screamed earthwards at full throttle. Forty-nine!

By this time, the Germans were queuing up for a shot at Barker's twisting aircraft. Bullets crackled round his ears and ripped savagely through the Snipe's wings and fuselage. Two Fokkers attacked simultaneously from behind. Barker throttled back and hammered one of them as it flashed past. The enemy shuddered and fell away, minus its tail. Fifty!

Then another Fokker zoomed up from below and fired a long burst into the underside of the Snipe. Bullets shattered Barker's left leg and he blacked out. The Snipe nosed over into a dive, and the rush of icy air brought the pilot round. At 12,000 feet, he managed to pull the aircraft out of its plunge towards the shell-scarred earth. The Snipe creaked and groaned alarmingly, and smoke poured from its overworked engine.

A Fokker came hurtling towards him, head-on. Weak from loss of blood, with both his legs smashed, Barker decided to ram it. Then, almost at the last moment, he saw an opportunity and opened fire. The effect was dramatic. The Fokker disintegrated in a cloud of blazing fragments. Miraculously, Barker flew unscathed through the whirling wreckage. Fifty-one!

Through a haze of pain, Barker realized that his left arm was useless. He looked down and saw that his sleeve was soaked with blood. A bullet had shattered his elbow. For the second time in this incredible one-sided battle, Barker fainted.

Again, it was the rush of the slipstream that brought him to his senses. The Fokkers were still boring in from all sides, determined to finish him off. Barker had almost stopped caring; almost, but not quite. One more Fokker made a fatal mistake. Again the Snipe's twin Vickers chattered. Again a German pilot died. Again a Fokker crashed to earth trailing a plume of smoke. Fifty-two!

Then, suddenly, the sky was clear. The Fokkers had vanished. Far below, troops of a Highland division who had been watching the combat stood up in their trenches and cheered themselves hoarse. But for Bill Barker, the ordeal was by no means over. Ahead of him now lay a desperate battle for survival. He could move only his right arm; his legs were useless and he was completely unable to operate the rudder bar. Yet somehow, he managed to keep a firm grip on the stick as the tattered, smoking, oil-slicked wreck of his aircraft sank lower. The ground rushed to meet him and the wheels struck with a jarring crash. The Snipe bounced high in the air and fell on its back in a cloud of dust. By some miracle it failed to catch fire.

Soldiers pulled him from the wreckage alive, but only just. They looked at him in awe. In a battle lasting forty minutes, he had taken on at least sixty enemy fighters. Not only that: he had destroyed five of them.

Barker was still unconscious in Rouen hospital, hovering between life and death, when the Armistice of 11 November 1918 finally silenced the guns on the western front. He eventually went on to make a full recovery – and to stand before King George v to receive one of the best-earned Victoria Crosses in the history of air combat.

Like many other young men who were introduced to the heady tonic of flying over the battlegrounds of Flanders, Bill Barker could not tolerate the idea of a job on the ground after the war. Flying continued to be his life. He became a test pilot, and in 1930, at the age of thirty-six, he was killed while flying the prototype of a new aircraft.

Death in the air and Bill Barker, vc, had kept a long-postponed rendezvous.

9 Billy Bishop: Canada's Ace

The little Nieuport fighter droned over the front line at 5000 feet, its blue-painted nose pointed steadily towards the east and the first streaks of dawn that were spreading over the horizon. In the narrow cockpit, Captain William Avery Bishop felt a strange sense of peace and isolation; the ugly scars of trenches and shell-craters were still hidden in the deep shadows far below, and it was hard to believe that in just a few more minutes he could be fighting desperately for his life. For, as the sun rose on this morning of 2 June 1917, Billy Bishop was about to put into practice the most audacious plan of his already spectacular flying career. It involved finding a German airfield while all the enemy aircraft were still on the ground – and then shooting them down, one by one, as they took off to attack him.

As the sun climbed higher details on the ground became more distinct, and some distance ahead of him Bishop picked out the grass airfield that was his target. On arriving overhead, however, he was seized by bitter disappointment; the place seemed to be completely deserted, with no sign of either aircraft or personnel.

Determined not to give up, Bishop turned south-east, intent on finding another field. He found one after a few more minutes, some twelve miles behind the lines near

Cambrai, and to his delight saw the sun glinting on a line of half a dozen Albatros fighters, some with their engines running. Putting his Nieuport into a shallow dive, he came down to 300 feet and sped towards his target. He crossed the airfield boundary at only fifty feet and opened fire, seeing the white faces of the German mechanics upturned as he streaked over their heads.

As he turned to make another run, machine-guns opened up from a series of nests around the airfield and punched holes in his wings, but Bishop knew that there was no turning back now. One of the enemy aircraft was beginning to take off and he closed in behind it just as it got airborne, firing a short burst of only fifteen rounds from dead astern. It went into a side-slip and crashed. Hauling the Nieuport round in a steep turn, his wing-tip almost brushing the grass, Bishop came in behind a second Albatros whose wheels had just left the ground. The German pilot pushed his nose down in a frantic effort to gain speed, glancing over his shoulder at the fighter rapidly overhauling him. A second later, just as Bishop opened fire, the German crashed headlong into a row of trees and blew up.

Looking round, Bishop felt his heart sink. Two more German machines had managed to take off and were now climbing away, apparently intent on boxing him in. Then, for some reason, he saw that only one enemy fighter was coming at him; the other was climbing in the opposite direction. The first Albatros caught up with Bishop and the two circled each other warily at 1000 feet, each seeking to gain a slight advantage. Bishop's turns were tighter, and he saw his opponent's tail gradually creep into his sights. A short, deadly burst of fire, and it was all over; the Albatros crashed on the airfield in a tangle of debris.

The other Albatros, meanwhile, had taken advantage of Bishop's involvement to gain height, and now he was coming in to the attack. Bishop turned to meet him and emptied his last drum of ammunition into him. If the German had pressed home his attack at this point Bishop would have stood no chance, but fortunately the enemy pilot lost his nerve and broke off the fight.

The danger, however, was by no means over. Bishop was now the target of every gun on and around the airfield, and he could see more enemy aircraft taking off to intercept him. With no time to waste, he put down the nose of his machine and headed flat out for friendly territory. He was almost completely exhausted, and when he saw four more enemy scouts overhead he knew it was the end; he had no more ammunition and precious little fuel to take evasive action. But the enemy pilots never saw him and he crossed the lines safely to regain his base. Only when he staggered from the cockpit did he realize the full extent of the punishment his Nieuport had taken. There were at least a hundred bullet holes in its wings and fuselage, but amazingly no vital spot had been hit. Bishop's daring had paid off, and his exploit was to earn him the Victoria Cross.

The basis of Bishop's prowess as an air fighter had been laid years earlier, in the woods around Owen Sound, Ontario, where he was born. It was there that he first learned to handle a rifle and shoot expertly, and after three years in Canada's Royal Military College at Kingston he had become an expert shot from horseback – so learning the techniques of deflection shooting that are so important in air combat.

At the end of his three years at Kingston, by which time war had broken out, Bishop – with a lieutenant's pips on his shoulders – was sent to England for a period of further training before going on to France with his unit. To the young officer, eager for action, the exercises and manœuvres seemed endless. Then, one day, as he was shivering in icy drizzle on Salisbury Plain, he looked up to see an aircraft humming overhead. 'It landed unhesitatingly in a nearby field,' he wrote later, 'as if scorning to brush its wings against so sordid a landscape, then away again up into the clean grey mists. How long I stood there gazing into the distance I do not know, but when I turned to slog my way back through the mud my mind was made up. I was going to meet the enemy in the air.'

On his next weekend leave in London Bishop went to the War Office and enquired about a transfer to the RFC. He was told that it would be easier to get in as an observer, so that he volunteered for this role – although his heart was still set on becoming a pilot. He was accepted and posted to France, where he spent four months on army co-operation work until a serious crash put him out of action with an injured knee. He was sent back to England to convalesce, and while he was there he lost no time in pressing forward his application for pilot training.

His persistence at last paid dividends, and in the middle of 1916 he found himself at a training school learning to fly Maurice Farman biplanes. He had considerable difficulty in mastering his new element, and his first solo flight was very nearly a disaster, but he improved steadily with perseverance and, after only fifteen hours' solo, was awarded his wings and posted to a home defence flight guarding the Thames Estuary against raiding Zeppelins. The unit was equipped with elderly BE2c biplanes, which were often incapable of climbing as high as the airships, and Bishop flew many night patrols without seeing one.

For a young man whose sole ambition was to be a single-seat fighter pilot, it was a terribly frustrating period, and he lodged several applications for a transfer to a scout unit in France. One of them found its way on to the right desk, and in March 1917 he went to France to join No. 60 Squadron, which was equipped with the latest Nieuports.

His early days with the squadron were hardly calcu-
lated to impress the veteran pilots in whose company
Bishop now found himself. On his second flight, he mis-
judged his landing badly and wrecked his aircraft. To
make matters worse, his squadron's commander had witnessed the whole incident and threatened to send the chas-
tened pilot back to England as unsuitable. Bishop turned
on all his charm and managed to win a second chance
for himself.

He had arrived at the front at a time when both sides
were struggling for air supremacy, and during the following weeks his squadron was to be involved in some desperate fighting. His first operational flight, on 25 March, involved escorting some bombers which were harrying German forces on their withdrawal to the Hindenburg Line;
it was very nearly his last. At 9000 feet in the Arras sector
his flight was attacked by three Albatros scouts. One of
them got on the tail of an aircraft ahead of Bishop and
the Canadian opened fire, at which the enemy aircraft
went into a steep dive to 6000 feet. Bishop followed him
down, firing in short bursts, and the battle descended to
2000 feet. He saw his bullets strike home and the Albatros
went into a spin. It had no hope of recovering before it
hit the ground.

Bishop's own engine, however, was misfiring badly, and
a few moments later it cut out altogether. Stretching his
glide as much as he dared, he managed to cross the front-
line trenches and made a rough landing beyond. He spent
the rest of the day, with the help of some soldiers, pushing
the Nieuport from one spot to another to prevent the
enemy artillery getting a fix on it. After dark he inspected
the engine and soon diagnosed the trouble: oily plugs. He
cleaned these thoroughly with the aid of a borrowed tooth-
brush, and at first light took off and flew back to base.

A week later, on 31 March, he destroyed his second

enemy aircraft. His colleagues on 60 Squadron were slowly beginning to realize that the newcomer had talent after all.

During April, as Canadian troops hurled themselves at Vimy Ridge, the pilots of 60 Squadron operated at maximum effort. Just before the offensive developed they were ordered to destroy a series of enemy observation balloons, and since these were protected by both heavy anti-aircraft-fire and fighters some violent action was usually the outcome. On 7 April Bishop was attacking one such balloon when he himself was attacked by an Albatros. He turned to meet the enemy aircraft and quickly shot it down, then turned his attention back to the balloon which was rapidly being hauled in. A few well-aimed bursts of tracer and the gas-bag burst into flames, whereupon Bishop turned for home. Then, once again, his engine cut out – and this time he was well inside enemy territory. He had just about resigned himself to becoming a prisoner when it started up again as his wheels were almost touching the ground. Feverishly, he regained altitude and reached home safely.

Young pilots of the Royal Flying Corps came to maturity quickly during that 'Bloody April' of 1917 – those, that is, who survived. Billy Bishop was one of the lucky ones. Conscious that his marksmanship in the air left much to be desired, despite his earlier expertise with a rifle, he set about improving it. He would fill his cockpit with tin cans, climb as high as his Nieuport would allow, then throw them out and shoot at them as they tumbled down. As his aim improved, so did his success in combat: in six weeks during April and May 1917 he shot down twenty enemy aircraft.

On 2 May a series of bitter air fights lasting all day earned him the award of the Distinguished Service Order. The drama he lived through is captured in his combat reports:

'At 9.50 at 13,000 NE of Monchy while returning from photographic escort, I attacked one single-seater HA (Hostile Aircraft) and fired two bursts of five rounds each. I was unable to catch him and evidently did not hit him.

'Later I saw five HA about 6000, doing artillery observation. I manœuvred to catch one party of three when just west of the Queant-Drocourt line, as that was the nearest they were coming to our lines. I attacked the rear one and after one burst of fifteen rounds, he fell out of control and crashed near Vitry, just east of Queant-Drocourt line. While watching him, another two-seater came up underneath me and opened fire. I attacked him firing about forty rounds. He fell out of control and I followed about 1500 feet, finishing my drum. He was in a spinning nose-dive and my shots could be seen entering all around the pilot's and observer's seats. Three more HA being above me, I returned.'

After refuelling and rearming, he was soon in the air once more.

'At 12.15 east of Lens 8000 feet I attacked two HA doing artillery observation, firing twenty rounds into one. They then escaped. Watching five minutes later, I saw only one HA there, the other evidently having been forced to land.

'At 12.35 east of Monchy at 6000 feet, I attacked two HA doing artillery observation, but only succeeded in driving them away. At 12.40 over Monchy at 9000 feet, I attacked from underneath a two-seater returning from our lines. I fired a whole drum into him but there was no apparent result. At 1.5 over Peloes at 6000 feet, I attacked the same two HA as above and fired a drum from long range. No apparent result. I returned to aerodrome as I had no more ammunition.'

After snatching a hasty lunch, Bishop took off for the third time that day.

'At 3.45 south of Vitry at 11,000 feet, while leading the offensive patrol I attacked two HA, firing into the rear one. He turned and I fired sixty rounds at him. He dived on me while I was correcting a stoppage. I then turned and finished my drum at him. I opened fire again from underneath, but he flew away and I was unable to overtake him. At 4.30 Wancourt, I attacked one HA from above, firing seventy rounds at him. He turned on me while I was changing my drum and I fired a whole drum with the exception of about five to ten rounds at him. At 5 pm I fired the remainder from long range at six HA attacking one of our machines.

In all, during that hectic day, Bishop had taken on twenty-three enemy aircraft and had shot down two of them, damaging others. The feat was characteristic of him; like Albert Ball before him he was a lone wolf, relying on aggressive tactics and the quick, deadly thrust to see him through. As his success grew, so did his obsession to achieve a record number of kills, as he freely admitted:

'I had become very ambitious, and was hoping to get a large number of machines officially credited to me.... With this object in view I planned many little expeditions of my own, and, with the use of great patience, I was very successful in one or two.'

One such expedition was the attack on the German airfield on 2 June, shortly after Bishop had returned to the front after a spell of leave. After that, he flew to his absolute limit, seized with a grim determination to add to his score every time he took to the air. On one occasion he carried out six patrols without scoring any kills, even though his machine was riddled with holes as a result of the fights he had experienced. Not content, he took off yet again in the late afternoon, and shortly afterwards sighted a lone Albatros at 5000 feet over Armentieres. Elated, he dived towards it, intent on a kill.

In his enthusiasm he had forgotten one of the basic rules of air fighting: he had neglected to look behind. Had he done so he would have seen five more Albatros, coming down fast out of the clouds. Nevertheless, they could not intervene in time to save their lone companion; Bishop's first burst sent it down in flames. Alert now to the danger behind, Bishop turned to meet it, racing head-on for the leading German machine. At the last instant the German broke away; his turn was too steep and he flicked into a spin. Bishop saw him crash.

The Canadian latched on to the tail of another Albatros, opened fire – and his guns jammed. Not only was he now unarmed, but because his port aileron had been damaged earlier in the day he was having trouble in controlling his aircraft. But the Albatros, Bishop saw, was in an even worse state. Its starboard wing was ripped, with many of the struts shattered. In a flash, Bishop made up his mind what to do. Bringing his aircraft alongside the German, he edged closer until he got his port wing-tip under that of the Albatros – and then shoved the stick hard over to the right. There was a terrific jolt and his Nieuport skidded away violently, jerking and shuddering but still under control. The German was less fortunate; Bishop saw part of his wing tear away and he fluttered down to crash.

There was no sign of the other German machines. Bishop carefully nursed his aircraft home for a safe if erratic landing, satisfied at last with his day's work.

In 1918 Bishop was given command of his own squadron, No. 85. By the beginning of June his score had risen to forty-seven, and he was still as determined as ever to push it up to the highest possible level. Then came the blow. His superiors, deciding that his luck could not last for ever, decided to send him back to England in a fortnight's time.

During that fortnight, Bishop flew and fought as never before. In a period of twelve days, representing a total of only thirty-six and a half hours' flying time, he destroyed a further twenty-five enemy aircraft. On 17 June, his last day in action but one, he downed three machines in thirty minutes – and used just fifty-five rounds of ammunition in the process. Once again, his terse combat report describes the action:

'10.25 am. Staden and Hooglede. 18,000 feet.
  (i) Between Staden and Hooglede, 18,000 feet at 10.25 am, I turned back a two-seater who was approaching our lines, finally closing to seventy-five yards. After twenty rounds he burst into flames.

10.50 am. Sailly-sur-le-Lys. 4000 feet.
  (ii) Over Sailly-sur-le-Lys, 4000 feet at 10.50 am, seeing one Albatros I zoomed into the edge of a cloud. Albatros passed cloud and I secured position on tail. After fifteen rounds he fell and crashed just south of village.

10.55 am. Laventie (near). 2000 feet.
  (iii) After attacking (ii) I saw a two-seater EA quite low. I dived at him from the east but he turned and got east of me. After second burst of twenty rounds he fell in a turning dive, then crashed between Laventie and main road.'

The next day, his last, was even more dramatic. Patrolling near Ypres, he saw and attacked three Pfalz fighters, one of which he quickly sent down in flames. As the others turned to attack him, two more Pfalz dropped down from the clouds to join the fray. For a few minutes the five machines circled, the Germans waiting for a chance to get in a killing burst. Then, as two of the Pfalz turned towards him, Bishop acted like lightning. He dived between them and the two enemy aircraft, tightening their turns, collided with one another and fluttered down in a cloud of wreckage. The other two immediately broke and fled; Bishop went after them, opening fire on one from 200 yards. The Pfalz went down and burst into flames. The sole survivor, to Bishop's annoyance, escaped in a cloud.

The next day, Bishop left France for good. In just over a year of air combat, he had sent seventy-two enemy aircraft to destruction. In this top-scoring bracket, only he and one other pilot – the Frenchman, René Fonck – were destined to survive the war.

During the Second World War, Bishop – now an Air Marshal – was placed in charge of recruiting for the Royal Canadian Air Force. For this work he received the CB to add to his already impressive list of decorations. He died of an illness on 11 September 1956.

10 Roderic Dallas: Bomber Destroyer

The big twin-engined *Friedrichshafen* bombers droned steadily over the drab Belgian landscape, heading for their bases deep behind the German lines. Although this was 20 May 1916, and summer warmth had begun to touch the battlefields far below, the bomber crews were frozen stiff at the end of their flight across the English Channel. Their target had been Dover, and on the way back they had dropped the last of their bombs on Dunkirk, which was one of the principal supply bases for the British Expeditionary Force.

As the bombers passed Blankenberghe, a solitary pair of eyes followed their progress. For several minutes Captain Roderic Dallas had been shadowing the five-strong enemy formation in his little Nieuport 'Baby' fighter, slipping in and out of cloud a thousand feet higher up. Although he knew that the bombers were heavily armed, he reckoned that if he could break up their tight formation he might be able to pick them off one by one.

Pushing down the nose of his Nieuport he raced through the middle of the enemy formation, guns hammering, then pulled up in a steep climb to gain height before repeating the process. As he had expected, the formation started to break up and lose its cohesion as the bomber pilots took evasive action. Fastening himself to the tail of a straggler,

Dallas exchanged fire with the German gunner and saw the man collapse as bullets hit him. Another burst shattered the *Friedrichshafen*'s port engine and pieces of strut flew back in the slipstream. Ponderously, the bomber lurched into a spin and went down, burning like a torch.

Dallas immediately closed in behind a second bomber, raking it and then shooting past. Turning steeply, he came in for a frontal attack, his bullets chewing up the enemy's cockpit. This bomber too caught fire and began to go down, trailing a dense banner of smoke and breaking up as it fell. Dallas, low on fuel and out of ammunition, broke off the fight and returned to base, well satisfied with his effort.

It was nearly two years since Dallas had left his native Australia, arriving in England as a second lieutenant shortly after the outbreak of war with one of the first contingents of Australian troops earmarked for service on the western front. Right from the start, the twenty-three-year-old officer had one ambition: to fly. Numerous applications to join the Royal Flying Corps, however, met with no success, and in 1915 he changed his tactics and applied to join the Royal Naval Air Service. This time, he was accepted.

On completion of his flying training he was posted to No. 1 Squadron RNAS, which was based at Dover and equipped with Short seaplanes. Its primary task was to patrol the Channel and North Sea Coast and Dallas found the work infinitely boring. Then, in the autumn of 1915, several RNAS squadrons were sent to France to assist the Royal Flying Corps, which was beginning to suffer heavy losses at the hands of the enemy's new Fokker monoplane. No. 1 Squadron, which moved to Dunkirk, was allocated several Nieuports – nimble little machines with an 80-hp engine and a Lewis gun mounted on top of the wing.

Dallas was delighted with the new aircraft, which was far superior to the seaplanes he had been used to.

It was now, during his patrols over the Dunkirk sector, that the flying experience gained by Dallas in his long hours over the sea in all weathers paid dividends. His first success came on 12 May 1916, when he caught an Aviatik two-seater over the front line. Closing right in, he aimed for the Aviatik's cockpit and opened fire in short, deadly bursts, killing or wounding the enemy pilot and gunner. The Aviatik went out of control and fluttered down to crash.

On the twenty-first, the day after his exploit against the big *Friedrichshafens*, he was airborne again to intercept an Albatros two-seater which was attempting to bomb Dunkirk. Dallas shot it down in flames. The next day, accompanied by a pilot named Lieutenant Mulock, he attacked a formation of three Albatros in the same area. Dallas shot down one and Mulock accounted for the other two, all in the space of a few minutes. Soon afterwards, Dallas was awarded the first of his decorations for gallantry – the Distinguished Service Cross.

The Germans were learning their lesson, and now they began to send their bomber and observation aircraft into the Dunkirk sector escorted by Fokkers. On 9 June, while carrying out a defensive patrol, Dallas sighted a small formation of LVGs escorted by fighters, and since he had a height advantage he decided to attack. Coming down fast behind the enemy formation, he was on the bombers before the escorting Fokkers had a chance to react. He poured fire into a fuselage of an LVG and its tail broke away, the front section – with the cockpit containing the luckless occupants – spiralling down.

Glancing back hastily, Dallas saw a Fokker coming down after him. He turned to meet the enemy, fired, and the Fokker fell apart. The other enemy fighters milled about in confusion, and Dallas saw his opportunity to escape.

Two days later, on the eleventh, Dallas engaged another formation of bombers escorted by Fokkers. This time, the German fighter pilots were fully alert and attacked the Australian as he approached the bombers, shooting up his Nieuport badly. His engine was hit, and he knew that he had to get down quickly before he was shot out of the sky. As he searched desperately for somewhere to land, a Fokker came down on his tail and opened fire, punching bullets through his wings. Dallas should have been finished – but the German pilot had made a bad error of judgement. His high speed caused him to overshoot, and as he flashed over the top of the Nieuport Dallas fired a burst into his underside from the Lewis gun, which was mounted on a swivel. His aim was excellent; the Fokker burst into flames and went down. Dallas swivelled his gun again and fired at a second fighter. Once again his aim was deadly and the Fokker plunged earthwards, minus a wing. A couple of minutes later Dallas made a successful forced landing behind the Allied lines.

At the end of 1916 No. 1 Squadron moved to Chapilly to form part of the 14th Army Air Wing and began to re-equip with a new aircraft type: the Sopwith Triplane. An excellent and manœuvrable machine, the triplane equipped six RNAS squadrons serving on the western front, and was more than a match for the Albatros DI and DII fighters which the Germans were then bringing into service.

The triplane-equipped squadrons were to play a major part during the intense air fighting of April 1917, and Dallas excelled in the violent action of this period. On 21 April, while patrolling with Lieutenant Culling, he sighted a pair of enemy two-seater observation aircraft and decided to attack, although they were strongly escorted by Albatros DIIs. The two triplanes ripped into the enemy formation and a furious dogfight ensued. Out of the corner of his eye, Dallas saw Culling hit one Albatros with a good burst; the wings of the enemy fighter folded up and it plummeted down. An instant later, Dallas fired at a second Albatros which appeared in front of him in a steep climb. The fighter hung poised for an instant, as though clawing the air with its propeller, then burst into flames.

In the resulting confusion the two triplane pilots made a beeline for the observation aircraft. Dallas fired at one, and it began to stream a ribbon of white vapour. A split second later it exploded and rolled earthwards, a ball of flame. One crew member, his clothing on fire, jumped clear and fell like a stone. Culling, meanwhile, shot up the other two-seater, which went down out of control. Both triplanes then headed away from the scene as fast as they could, ripped and torn by enemy bullets. Both were wrecked on landing, but their pilots escaped with only a few bruises. The fight earned Dallas a Mention in Despatches and the award of the French *Croix de Guerre*.

By the end of May the Allied air forces had succeeded in achieving local air superiority and were now going over to the offensive on all sectors of the front. For Dallas, one of the most hectic days was 22 June; during his first morning patrol he ripped through six enemy fighters to shoot down the AEG observation aircraft they were escorting, escaping without damage to his own machine, and soon after midday he destroyed a similar aircraft. On this occasion the AEG did not appear to be escorted, but Dallas should have known better. As he climbed away from his kill, he looked behind and saw five Halberstadt fighters descending on him. The Germans split up, one machine turning ahead of Dallas to cut off his escape and divert his attention from two more who had dived to get underneath him. Dallas gave the Halberstadt in front of him a long burst and saw the pilot slump in the cockpit. The machine went out of control and fell away beneath the triplane, narrowly missing the other two Halberstadts who broke wildly to get out of its way. Seizing his chance, Dallas shot up into a cloud and made his escape.

A couple of weeks later Dallas was appointed CO of No. 1 Squadron, which moved to Bailleul in support of the 3rd Army. During the last half of the year the squadron fought against some of Germany's best fighter units, including the Richthofen *Geschwader*, and under Dallas's leadership the triplane pilots proved more than capable of holding their own. In the autumn the triplanes, which had given such faithful service, were replaced by Sopwith Camels, and by the end of 1917 Dallas had brought his score of confirmed victories up to twenty-six while flying this type of aircraft.

In March 1918 he was given a new command: No. 40 Squadron. He quickly found himself in the thick of more heavy fighting, for during the next few weeks the squadron – equipped with SE5s – carried out intensive ground-attack work in support of the British 3rd and 4th Armies, reeling under the shock of the Ludendorff offensive. Losses were high, and early in April Dallas came very close to losing his life when his aircraft was badly hit by machine-gun fire from the ground. Although wounded in both legs he managed to reach base safely. He was back in action a fortnight later, his legs still bandaged.

His score rose steadily during May, and by the twenty-eighth it had reached a total of thirty-nine enemy aircraft destroyed. Dallas, always in the thick of the fighting, was well known to the enemy, and the aircraft he flew was conspicuous. Instead of the drab khaki upper surfaces and cream underside that was the standard British colour scheme, he had it painted in a distinctive green and brown pattern resembling the pattern the Royal Air Force was to adopt many years later.

On 1 June 1918 Dallas set out on another of his lone patrols, intending to lurk in the sun over the front line and trap an unsuspecting enemy observation aircraft. He never returned. Later, his wrecked aircraft was found near the village of Lieven.

A German account later told the story of Dallas's last minutes. It appeared that he had dived down to attack a solitary Fokker triplane, unaware that two more were cruising several thousand feet higher up, waiting for just this moment. A long dive, a flurry of tracer, and the SE had gone down, its pilot shot through by a score of bullets.

This time, for Roderic Dallas, the man who had cheated death a dozen times in the face of impossible odds, there had been no way out.

11 Lufbery – the Tactician

For Raoul Lufbery, life was one long adventure – and flying was the greatest adventure of all. Born in France, Lufbery had emigrated to the United States with his parents and had grown to manhood there, becoming an American citizen and eventually joining the United States Army. Finding the rigid discipline of army life irksome, he left at the earliest opportunity and set out to see the world, travelling round the Far East.

His wanderings took him to Calcutta, where he met a French pilot named Marc Pourpe. Like Lufbery, Pourpe was a confirmed wanderer; he had learned to fly, bought himself one of Henri Farman's early biplanes, and had set off to tour the world in it, giving flying lessons and joy-rides to anyone who was willing to pay the necessary money. Lufbery was fascinated by this flamboyant character and the two became good friends, the American taking on the post of Pourpe's mechanic. Before long Lufbery too had learned to fly, and for the next couple of years the two travelled through India, China and Japan, giving flying demonstrations to enthusiastic audiences. Early in 1914 they went to Egypt, and Pourpe made history by carrying out a record non-stop flight from Cairo to Khartoum.

By this time their original aircraft was practically worn

out, so in the summer of 1914 they went to France with the intention of buying a new one. They were still there in August, when France and Germany went to war.

Pourpe immediately enlisted in the *Aviation Militaire*, where his flying skills would be put to good use. Lufbery, however, had a problem in that he was an American citizen, and as such could not join the French armed forces. There was one loophole, and Lufbery quickly found it. He joined the French Foreign Legion, automatically becoming a French citizen for the duration of his service, and soon afterwards he applied for a transfer to the Air Arm. He put in a request to become Pourpe's mechanic, and to his delight it was granted.

When Pourpe was killed towards the end of 1914, Lufbery felt a deep sense of loss and a desire to avenge his friend. He at once applied for pilot training, and during the first half of 1915 he learned to fly the clumsy Maurice Farmans and Voisins that every embryo French pilot had to master before going on to greater things. Lufbery's early flying career was far from spectacular; in fact his performance indicated that he was not suited to handling light and manœuvrable aircraft such as single-seat scouts, and his instructors said that he lacked the finesse that was necessary to become a really proficient pilot. Nevertheless, he got through his course and was awarded his wings – but when his posting came through it was to a bomber squadron, not the single-seat unit on which he had set his heart. It was a bitter disappointment, but he had no choice other than to bear it.

Several other Americans were also serving in the French Air Arm, having enlisted by the same devious method as Lufbery, and although the French were grateful for their help they were not eager to advertise their presence, for the United States was neutral and there was always the possibility of diplomatic repercussions. In Paris, however, there lived a man who had a dream: it was to see all these young Americans banded together in one unit, fighting for the cause of liberty rather than the French High Command.

His name was Edmund L. Gros, and he was a doctor of medicine who had been practising in Paris for many years. His patriotism was shared more or less equally between the United States and France, and his ideals had a sound backing of influence and wealth. Gros had already helped to form an American Ambulance Service in France during the first months of the war, and now, in the autumn of 1915, he turned his attention to the formation of an all-American air squadron.

Such a plan had, in fact, been in existence for some time. It had been originated by a young pilot named Norman Prince, of Pride's Crossing in Massachusetts, who had already done a great deal to clear many of the diplomatic obstacles out of the way. Prince came to Paris and teamed up with Gros, and soon they were joined by other influential Americans living in Paris. Together, they started a recruiting campaign combing the Foreign Legion, the Ambulance Service and the French forces in search of Americans who might be willing to volunteer for flying duties. As soon as a likely candidate was located, and showed willing, Gros had him transferred to the French Air Arm for training; this step was accomplished with the help of one Jarousse de Silac, a senior member of the French War Ministry, who believed wholeheartedly in the Americans' scheme.

As soon as the American airmen completed their training they were posted to various air units for operational service, while Gros and his colleagues worked hard behind the scenes to obtain official approval for the formation of the American squadron. The word spread quickly and more volunteers began to arrive from the United States, some of them having already tried to join the Royal Flying Corps. In the spring of 1916 they were all either operational or under training in France, awaiting the call from Gros and Prince.

It came on 17 April 1916. On that day the '*Escadrille Americaine*' – known officially as *Escadrille* N124 within the French Air Arm – was formed around a nucleus of seven pilots, with Norman Prince at their head. During the next few days seven more arrived, having been detached from their respective French units. Among them was Raoul Lufbery.

The *Escadrille* moved up to Bar-le-Duc, in the Verdun sector, and its pilots – many of whom had already acquired considerable operational experience with the French – soon began to distinguish themselves. During the next five months they took part in 156 air combats and officially destroyed seventeen enemy aircraft; they had also suffered their first casualties, among them Norman Prince, who was killed when his aircraft crashed on landing at night. And Raoul Lufbery, the man whose instructors had said was not sufficiently competent to fly fighter aircraft, was slowly emerging as one of the best pilots of them all.

Late in 1916 the *Escadrille* moved to the Somme sector. By this time its fighting prowess was so well established that the German Government had lodged a protest with the United States against the Escadrille's existence, claiming that the word 'Americaine' in its title was a violation of the USA's neutrality. The French government accordingly decided to change the title to the *Escadrille Lafayette*, the name recalling the French soldier and nobleman who had fought for the Americans in the War of Independence.

By the time the United States entered the war in 1917, the score of the *Escadrille Lafayette* stood at 199 enemy aircraft. Although the American Air Service began to establish itself in France at the beginning of 1918, and although the American airmen already in action were transferred to it on paper, with US Army ranks, there was no rapid transfer of personnel to form new American air units. The Americans had no shortage of manpower; their physical requirements were high, and – incredible though it may seem – some of the men who had fought so well with the *Escadrille Lafayette* were found to be below the required standard.

Raoul Lufbery, who now had seventeen victories to his credit, was commissioned into the American Air Service in January 1918. He now had the rank of Major, and expected to receive orders to form an American squadron. Instead, to his disgust, he was sent to the training school at Issoudun, where recruits to the Air Service were knocked into shape before starting their flying courses. For three months he chafed at his enforced lack of activity, until at last – in April – he was posted as an instructor to the 94th Squadron in the Champagne sector. Together with its sister squadron, the 95th, this unit made up the American First Pursuit Group.

For the next few weeks, Lufbery threw himself into the task of bringing the 94th's pilots up to operational standard. At the same time, he fought one battle after another with the authorities in an effort to ensure that the squadron received the equipment it needed. By the middle of April, for example, the squadron's Nieuport fighters still had no guns, which meant that Lufbery could not lead his pilots over the lines. It seemed that some supply officer, somewhere in the rear area, deemed the issue of socks more important than the issue of weapons. In the end Lufbery went straight to General Pershing, the American Air Service commander – and the guns arrived in record time after that.

Lufbery could now take his men for a look at the other side, having taught them all he knew about air fighting

tactics. Like Mick Mannock, he shepherded them carefully, making sure they did not stray out of formation. On
returning to base, he would get them to describe what they
had seen. He would then proceed to tell them all the things
they had missed, including aircraft that had passed them
by at a distance of only a few hundred yards. In this way
he taught them to keep a good look-out, and as the days
went by their perception became as good as his own.

At last Lufbery judged that his pilots were ready to go
into action on their own, and on 18 April three Nieuport
Scouts of the 94th Squadron were detailed to carry out
the First Pursuit Group's first combat patrol. It was
led by Captain David Petersen, with Lieutenants Reed
Chambers and Edward Rickenbacker as his wingmen.
The patrol was uneventful and the three pilots returned
to their airfield. Soon after they had landed, however, two
German aircraft were reported in the area. Two more
American pilots, Lieutenants Alan Winslow and Douglas
Campbell, immediately took off and each shot down
an enemy machine – the first air victories credited to an
American squadron.

Lufbery's training schedule was not confined to work
in the air. He was always available whenever his pilots
wanted his advice, and he would spend long hours with
them in the evenings, discussing tactics with them. His
method of fighting was much the same as Mannock's:
approach with caution and make sure the odds are in your
favour before committing yourself. Above all, he told
them, keep a cool head. Panic was the fighter pilot's worst
enemy. If your aircraft is set on fire, he advised, side-slip
to keep the flames away from the cockpit and get down
as quickly as you can. That way, you have at least some
chance of survival; you have none at all if you panic and
jump clear.

Lufbery and Mannock, in fact, had a great deal in common besides their approach to the science of air combat. Both were adored by their pupils, who thought them invincible; both knew that their luck could not last forever. Lufbery, during the earlier stages of his flying career, had made friends with many French pilots, and had seen them die one after the other. He knew that, by the law of averages, his own turn must come soon.

Raoul Lufbery's luck finally ran out on 19 May 1918. During a fight with an Albatros right over the 94th's airfield at Toul, his Nieuport was hit and set on fire. In full view of the horrified Americans on the ground, it nosed down and was soon enveloped in flames. Like a fiery torch, it descended through 400–300–200 feet, and the agony of the man in the cockpit was not hard to imagine. Then the witnesses saw a dark shape detach itself and plummet to earth. The flames had won their battle, and Lufbery had jumped. They found his body in a garden on the outskirts of Nancy.

12 Eddie Rickenbacker: America's Top-Scorer

In the spring of 1918 another of Anthony Fokker's amazing designs once again threatened the air superiority that had been achieved by the Allies at the cost of much blood and sweat during the previous months, just as his little EIII monoplane had done three years earlier. His new creation was the Fokker DVII, hailed by many as the best German fighter of the First World War. Armed with two Spandau machine-guns, it had an excellent performance at high altitude and could climb to 16,000 feet in under half an hour, giving it the edge over most Allied types.

Von Richthofen's *Jagdgeschwader* 1 was the first to receive the new type in April 1918, at the time of the Baron's death, and other leading fighter units rapidly re-equipped with it. In August alone, the DVII-equipped squadrons destroyed no fewer than 560 Allied aircraft.

This was the fighter most frequently encountered in the summer of 1918 by the American First Pursuit Group, which had now expanded into five squadrons: the 94th, 95th, 27th, 147th and 185th, the latter reserved for night fighting. The Group's Spads had a hard time of it, and it took a very capable pilot to master this new and redoubtable enemy.

One such was Captain Eddie Rickenbacker, one of the pilots who had carried out the Group's first war patrol on 18 April. When the United States entered the war in 1917 he had been one of America's leading racing drivers, earning 40,000 dollars a year; his name then was spelt Richenbacher, which he quickly changed to the more American-sounding version as a tide of anti-German feeling swept the nation. He enlisted at once in the American Air Service and underwent a primary flying course, but his subsequent flying career was almost ruined by the fact that he was an excellent engineer; on arrival at Issoudun, the American flying school in France, he was immediately put in charge of the engineering section and made responsible for repairs and modifications to the aero-engines of training machines.

He repeatedly requested a transfer to a fighting squadron, but his superiors blocked him at every turn; at twenty-eight, they said, he was too old to fly in combat. Nevertheless he persevered, flying at every opportunity and improving his techniques largely by trial and error without the benefit of much advanced instruction. His fast reactions and his ability to judge speeds and distances, qualities that had enabled him to shine as a racing driver, now proved invaluable in the air; without them he would probably have killed himself. Conditions at Issoudun were bad; there was churned-up mud everywhere, and fatal accidents on take-off or landing were frequent. Sometimes, earth, mud or loose stones found their way into engines, which subsequently failed after take-off with disastrous results.

It was General Pershing, commanding the American forces in France, who lifted Rickenbacker out of the rut and had him transferred to his headquarters in Paris for duty as a driver. One day, Rickenbacker was driving two of Pershing's senior air staff officers, Colonel Billy Mitchell and Major Townsend Dodd, on a tour of inspection around the American air bases when their car broke down. Rickenbacker quickly repaired the damage, and the two officers were impressed by his expertise; so much, in fact, that Mitchell remembered the incident when Rickenbacker's next application for a posting to combat duty arrived on his desk and placed his stamp of approval on it.

So it came about that Rickenbacker's cherished dream at last became reality, and in March 1918 he was posted to the 94th Squadron under Raoul Lufbery. With Lufbery's teaching and his own natural flying ability he soon began to show promise, excelling particularly in team fighting. His first team-mate was a young pilot called Norman Hall, and Rickenbacker scored his first kill while flying with him. Then Hall was shot down and taken prisoner, and soon afterwards Rickenbacker was made a Flight Commander.

For some time, Rickenbacker had been troubled with earache, but he had put it down to a cold draught in the cockpit and had not paid much attention to it. Then, one day, he developed a raging fever. It grew steadily worse, and he was sent back to Paris for a thorough medical examination. The doctors found that he had mastoiditis, and decided to operate immediately. Rickenbacker made a full recovery, but he was out of action for two months.

He found great changes on his return to the squadron. Several of his old friends had been killed, wounded or taken prisoner, and losses continued to mount as the new and deadly Fokkers outflew and outfought the elderly Nieuports that equipped the American unit. Rickenbacker returned at a time when the Americans were literally fighting for survival; lessons in combat had to be learned the first time, because there was usually no second chance.

On one occasion, Rickenbacker was leading his flight of six Nieuports on an escort mission, protecting a pair of two-seaters which were photographing enemy troop movements in the Aisne sector, when the formation ran slap into the middle of a dogfight between some French Spads and Fokkers. A Fokker swept past Rickenbacker's nose and he fired, seeing his tracers strike home and the enemy aircraft begin its downward plunge, but the next instant he himself was fighting for his life as another Fokker latched on to his tail. Wildly, he put his machine into a spin and dropped for several hundred feet, finally levelling out just above the ground and speeding for home. On landing, he discovered that the Fokker's guns had punched a line of holes in his fuselage, just aft of the cockpit. He got his mechanics to patch them up and paint a miniature iron cross over each one, so that he would be reminded of the incident every time he climbed into his machine. He would not forget to look behind him in future.

Very quickly, Rickenbacker learned the essentials for staying alive. He learned, for example, that in a Nieuport it was suicidal to put oneself into a position where the only way out was by means of a steep dive: several pilots had been killed when the wings of their aircraft ripped away while carrying out this manœuvre. In a Nieuport you fought on the turn, taking full advantage of the little aircraft's manœuvrability.

He made a deep study of tactics, learning much from the combat careers and fighting methods of both Allied and enemy pilots. As far as he was concerned, the pilots of the Royal Flying Corps were the finest anywhere; their aggressive spirit was matched with a coolness of temperament that was second to none. Air war for them was a science, a cold, calculating business, and that was how Rickenbacker looked at it too. The RFC pilots were trained

113

to adapt themselves to any situation, no matter how un-
expected, and in this they differed from the Germans, who
tended to fight by the book, and the French, who generally
were over flamboyant. So, despite the American Group's
strong French connections, it was the lessons learned by
the British that became Rickenbacker's textbook, and he
passed them on faithfully to his subordinates.

In August 1918 the First Pursuit Group re-equipped
with Spads, and at last the Americans had a machine that
could hold its own against the Fokker DVII. Rickenbacker took to the Spad at once, being particularly
impressed by its fast rate of climb. He took one up and
put it through its paces, teaching himself its limitations
and advantages and working out a new range of combat
tactics to go with it.

A couple of weeks later, in September, Rickenbacker
was appointed to command the 94th Squadron. It was a
bold decision on the part of his superiors, because other
Flight Commanders were senior to him; nevertheless, his
all-round experience matched that of most others, and in
some aspects – such as technical skill – he excelled. He was
also a very fine leader, a man who took the utmost care
of the pilots he led into action and assumed personal
responsibility for getting them back safely. Everyone, from
mechanics upwards, openly worshipped this tall, rangy
man with the permanently crooked smile. Somehow, he
seemed a natural choice for command.

His superiors' faith in him was soon justified. He took
over command of the 94th at a time when there was keen
rivalry between it and its sister unit, the 27th Squadron,
and at the beginning of September the 27th had managed
to creep ahead in the number of victories scored. This was
a major source of annoyance to Rickenbacker, partly
because the 27th was a newer unit than his own, and his
first act on taking over was to get all the squadron per-

sonnel together and deliver a strong pep talk. To the mechanics, he pointed out bluntly that the 27th's machines were seldom on the ground because of technical trouble, and that he expected to see a rapid rise in the standards of maintenance. From the pilots, he expected a comparable rise in the standard of tactics and teamwork; when they were not fighting they would train arduously until that standard had been reached.

It was tough stuff from a new commander, and had the words been delivered by anyone other than Rickenbacker they might have caused resentment. As it was, he achieved his object, and from that day the 94th set out to be better than any other unit. On the morning of 15 September, Rickenbacker hammered his point home in the best way he knew: he took off and shot down two Huns before breakfast.

During the next fourteen days Rickenbacker destroyed twelve Fokkers, ably demonstrating the Spad's ability in the hands of a competent pilot and finally wiping out the psychological damage that had been caused by the advent of the German fighters and their spate of early victories. His score continued to climb steadily, and by the first week in October he was ahead of any other American pilot. The 94th Squadron, too, had recaptured its lead and showed no sign of relinquishing it again.

At the end of October Rickenbacker had twenty-six confirmed victories to his credit, and about a dozen more unconfirmed enemy aircraft had fallen before his guns on the other side of the lines. If he had been permitted to range freely over the front, carrying the war into the enemy camp in the manner of Ball, Mannock and McCudden, there is little doubt that he would have doubled his score. But policy restricted the scope of American air operations and left little room for individualism.

Rickenbacker's achievement in the few short weeks of

his combat command was summed up admirably by General Mitchell, who wrote:

> 'Captain Rickenbacker furnished, by his example, an ideal squadron leader. He and the other three squadron commanders in the Group were the type of squadron commanders it was absolutely necessary to have in pursuit aviation. It is useless to send out from the rear officers to command squadrons who have not had experience at the front. It is absolutely essential that squadron commanders be experienced and daring pilots. It is their duty to lead their squadrons into battle and to furnish them always a most glorious and enviable example. Captain Rickenbacker obtained results himself and his pilots could not help but emulate him and do likewise. A squadron commander who sits in his tent and gives orders and does not fly, though he may have the brains of Solomon, will never get the results that a man will who, day in day out, leads his patrols over the line and infuses into his pilots the *esprit de corps* which is so necessary in aviation and which, so far, has been so lightly considered by the military authorities.'

The performance of the American Air Service in 1918 is testimony enough to the prowess of Rickenbacker and his fellow commanders in shaping a young, untrained force into a first-rate fighting body. The pilots of the First Pursuit Group alone shot down 285 enemy machines; it was no mean achievement for a fighting service which had entered combat three full years after its Allied contemporaries – and it laid a fine tradition which America's airmen were to sustain in a later conflict.

Eddie Rickenbacker survived the war to be feted back home as a national hero. He received America's highest award for gallantry: the Congressional Medal of Honor. It was to be bestowed on only one other American pilot in the First World War; a young man who was the opposite of Rickenbacker in every respect save courage and his skill in handling a fighter.

His name was Frank Luke.

13 The Boy from Arizona

It was 29 September 1918, and the great conflict that had claimed millions of lives over the past four years was nearing its end – although few realized it yet, including the German troops who manned the front-line trenches near the village of Murvaux, France. Faces upturned, they watched the lone aircraft that swept overhead, and then, as they recognized the distinctive snub-nosed outline of a French Spad fighter and the roundels on its wings, they opened fire with rifles and machine-guns.

The Spad flew on, apparently unharmed by the storm of fire, and headed for its target, three German observation balloons, which had been directing artillery fire on to Allied positions. Suddenly, the German soldiers' apprehension turned to cheers as ten Fokker DVII fighters came diving out of the sun. They had been patrolling at 12,000 feet, protecting the balloons, and now they savagely attacked the lone Spad.

Even the Germans had to admit that the Spad's pilot could handle his aircraft. For a good five minutes he twisted and turned, parrying every attack made on him by the Fokkers. Then, at last, the lone aircraft seemed to falter and spiral down, out of control.

A few moments later, the cheers of the German troops died away as the Spad suddenly righted itself and sped like an arrow for the nearest observation balloon. Its guns chattered briefly and the gas-bag burst into flames, collapsing as it fell. The Spad skimmed through the smoke and its guns rattled again, ripping the second balloon apart. On the ground, the German crew frantically began to haul in the third balloon, but it was far too late. That, too, went down in flames.

As the anti-aircraft fire redoubled in its intensity, the Spad stood on its wing-tip and came arrowing down towards the enemy gun positions, raking them with tracer. As it sped over them, its wheels almost brushing the sandbags, its pilot leaned over the edge of the cockpit and lobbed some hand grenades down on the heads of the startled gunners. Then he climbed steeply and turned to make another run.

At that moment the Spad wobbled as a solid burst of machine-gun fire hit it, wounding the pilot in the shoulder. Despite his injury the pilot made his second run, emptying his ammunition drum into the enemy trenches. Then, fighting to retain control, he cut his engine and side-slipped down to make a forced landing in a nearby field. The Spad rolled to a stop and the pilot climbed from the cockpit, leaning against the side of his machine as though overcome by an immense weariness. His injured arm hung limply by his side. With his other hand, he calmly and deliberately raised his ·45 revolver as German soldiers came running towards him. . . .

Here, in a muddy French field, the road was to end for Lieutenant Frank Luke, Jr, a year almost to the day after he left his native Arizona. During that year, he had carved out a reputation as a tough and fearless fighter; it had earned the admiration of both friend and enemy, and now, in these last few minutes of his life, it was to earn him his country's highest decoration for valour, the Congressional Medal of Honor.

He came from a tough background. As a youth he had ranged the Arizona mountains on foot, carrying a seventy-pound pack, and had worked in the rough, blow-for-blow world of a copper mine. With rifle and revolver he was unsurpassed, and with his inbred spirit of adventure it was hardly surprising that he had been among the first to volunteer for military service when America entered the war in 1917.

The life of an infantryman was not for Frank Luke. In September 1917 he enlisted in the Signal Corps and applied for assignment to the flying branch. He was quickly accepted and ordered to the School of Military Aeronautics at Austin, Texas, to undergo flying training. He proved an exceptional pilot right from the beginning, completing the normal nine-week course in seven weeks, and on 23 January 1918 he was commissioned as a Second Lieutenant in the Aviation Section, Signal Officers' Reserve Corps. Six weeks later, he left for France on active service.

After further training in France he was assigned to the 27th Aero Squadron, operating from a field near Chateau-Thierry. It was now the middle of August and Luke, eager for action, had not yet had so much of a glimpse of an enemy aircraft. After several uneventful patrols, he decided to set off alone and head for the one place where he could be sure of finding some opposition: a German airfield. After flying for some minutes, he spotted an airfield on the horizon – and a second or two later he saw something even more inviting, six Albatros fighters, flying in formation towards the very field he had picked out. His subsequent combat report tells the story of the encounter; the date was 16 August 1918.

'Saw Hun formation and followed, getting above, into the sun. The formation was strung out leaving one

machine way in the rear. Being way above the formation, I cut my motor and dove down on the rear man,
keeping the sun directly behind. Opened fire at about
a hundred feet, keeping both guns on him until to within
a few feet, then zoomed away. When I next saw him
he was on his back, but looked as though he was going
to come out of it, so I dove again, holding both guns
on him. Instead of coming out of it he side-slipped off
the opposite side, much like a falling leaf, and went
down on his back.

'My last dive carried me out of reach of another
machine that had turned about. They gave chase for
about five minutes, then turned back, for I was leading
them. My last look at the plane shot down convinced
me that he struck the ground, for he was still on his back
about 1,500 metres below.

'On coming home above our lines saw four EA.
Started to get into the sun and above, but they saw me
and dove towards me. I peaked for home. Three turned
back and the other came on. I kept out of range by peak-
ing slightly and he followed nearly to Coincy, where he
saw one of the 95th (Squadron) boys and turned about.
The 95th man could have brought down this EA if he
had realized quick enough that it was an EA....'

Because the aircraft shot down by Luke had fallen in
enemy territory, near Soissons, he could not claim it as
a victory, and in fact came in for a certain amount of ridi-
cule from his squadron mates when he pressed the claim.
In fact, his colleagues were not impressed by Luke at all
during those early days; he was too cocksure and arrogant
for their liking, and his squadron commander referred to
him on one occasion as 'the damndest nuisance that ever
stepped on to a flying field'. It only made Luke more determined than ever to excel, and he soon proved that he was

capable of doing it by making his speciality one of the most difficult and dangerous targets of all – the enemy observation balloons.

On 12 September the Americans launched a major offensive in the St Mihiel sector, and Luke's squadron was assigned to patrol a segment of the front. The pilots were briefed to look out for enemy observation aircraft and balloons, which were directing heavy and accurate artillery fire on to the American ground forces. Luke quickly spotted one of the balloons, floating about two miles inside the German lines, but since it was outside his patrol sector he left it alone at this stage, reporting its presence when he returned to base. He was told that several attacks had been made on it already by another squadron, which had suffered heavy losses in the process and met with no success.

Luke at once asked for permission to go after the balloon himself, and another pilot, Lieutenant Joe Wehner, volunteered to go along with him to protect him from enemy aircraft lurking up above and also to draw off some of the ground fire. The latter was formidable. Around each balloon – which was a big, sausage-shaped bag filled with hydrogen gas, floating at about 2000 feet on the end of a cable and carrying an observer suspended below it in a wicker basket – the Germans set up a ring of anti-aircraft and machine-guns. They set their shells to explode at the balloon's height, so that an attacker had to fly literally through a wall of shrapnel and machine-gun bullets. Once he got that far, a burst of incendiary bullets into the balloon's highly inflammable gas usually did the trick, but then the attacker had to fly through the fire sent up by the defences on the other side. It was small wonder that pilots hated balloon strafes; to volunteer for one was almost unheard of.

Nevertheless, Luke and Wehner set out in high spirits.

On sighting the balloon, Wehner broke off to provide top cover while Luke made his attack. Buffeted by shell bursts, Luke shot through the defensive ring and pressed the trigger – only to find that his guns had jammed. Undeterred, he climbed over the balloon, made a steep turn and came back again, flying the aircraft with one hand and clearing the stoppages with the other. This time, the guns worked and the balloon burst into flames, crumping up and falling while Luke dived for safety at high speed.

On the fourteenth, once again accompanied by Wehner, Luke set out to attack more balloons in the Buzy-Boinville sector. These balloons were sited in an area that provided excellent observation for the enemy, and were strung up at an unusually low altitude – so low, in fact, that their observers would be unable to use their recently-developed parachutes in the event of an attack. On the other hand, it was known that the balloons were even more stiffly defended than normal.

On this occasion, Luke and Wehner were escorted by a formation of six Spads, whose pilots were detailed to provide top cover. It was just as well, for the Fokkers were lurking up above, as Luke's combat report tells:

'... On arriving at Buzy, left formation and brought down enemy balloon in flames. While fixing my guns so I could attack another balloon nearby, eight enemy Fokkers dropped down on me. Pulled away from them. They scored several good shots on my plane. I saw Lieutenant Wehner dive through enemy formation and attack two enemy planes on my tail; but, as my guns were jammed, did not turn, as I was not sure it was an Allied plane until he joined me later....

'Left formation at Abaucourt and attacked an enemy balloon near Boinville. Dove at it six times at close range. Had two stoppages with left gun which carried incendiary bullets and, after fixing both, continued the attack. After about seventy-five rounds being left in right gun, I attacked an Archie battery at the base of the balloon. Am sure that my fire took effect as the crews scattered. After my first attack on the balloon the observer jumped after he shot at me. The last I saw of the balloon, it was on the ground in a very flabby condition.'

The German gunner who had fired back at Luke was Sergeant Münchhoff of the 14th Balloon Company. His companion, Signaller Gasser, had jumped a few seconds earlier. Miraculously, both their parachutes opened in the nick of time and they survived. Later, Münchhoff indicated that Luke could easily have shot him up as he descended, and in fact some of Luke's colleagues asked him why he had not done so. 'Hell,' was his reply, 'the bastard was helpless!' Ruthless in action Luke might have been, but he was no cold-blooded killer.

The next day, Luke and Wehner were ordered to bring down yet another balloon in the Boinville sector. As soon as they were over the front line they decided to split up and make a morning of it by shooting down as many balloons as their ammunition would allow, although these tactics ran contrary to their orders. North-east of Verdun Wehner attacked a balloon and set it on fire with a hundred rounds before diving away for his life with five Fokkers on his tail. They chased him as far as Chambley, when he was saved by the intervention of a group of French Spads. Wehner then turned towards the Bois d'Hingry, where another balloon had been reported, but before he could get there he saw it burst into flames and go down; Frank Luke had arrived ahead of him.

Nevertheless, Wehner's arrival on the scene was timely, for Luke's aircraft suddenly burst out of the smoke of the

falling balloon hotly pursued by seven Fokkers and Albatros DVs. Wehner came in behind Luke's attackers and
shot one down before the Germans realized he was there;
as they broke in all directions he loosed off another burst
into an Albatros, seeing it go into a steep dive and crash.
Chased by the remaining enemy fighters, the two Americans pushed their noses down and raced for safety.

Luke was off again that same afternoon, this time on
his own, although he was supposed to make rendezvous
with an escort over the front line.

'Patrolled to observe enemy activity. Left a little after
formation, expecting to find it on the lines. On arriving
there I could not find formation but saw artillery firing
on both sides. Also saw a light at about 500 metres. At
first I thought it was an observation machine but on
nearing it I found that it was a Hun balloon, so I
attacked and destroyed it. I was Archied with white fire,
and machine-guns were very active. Returned very low.
Saw thousands of small lights in woods north of Verdun.
On account of darkness coming on I lost my way and
landed in a French wheat field at Agers. . . .'

So far, every balloon strafe carried out by Luke had
resulted in more or less severe damage to his aircraft, and
to make matters more difficult – as he found on the morning of the sixteenth – the Germans had begun to haul in
their balloons as soon as an Allied aircraft was reported
crossing the front line. After giving some thought to the
problem, Luke and Wehner decided to make their attacks
at dusk, while the enemy observers were taking a last look
at the situation. That evening, the pair took off at 6.45,
and twenty minutes later their colleagues on the ground,
straining their eyes towards the east, suddenly saw the sky
glow red as the first balloon went down. Two more glows
during the next twenty minutes signified the destruction

of a second and third balloon. With the aid of flares, both Luke and Wehner landed safely.

Bad weather brought a halt to air operations on the seventeenth, but in the late afternoon of the next day Luke and Wehner were airborne again in search of new victims. In the terse words of Luke's combat report:

'Lieutenant Wehner and I left the airdrome at sixteen hours to spot enemy balloons. Over St Mihiel we saw two German balloons near Labeuville. Maneuvred in the clouds and dropped down, burning both. We were then attacked by a number of EA, the main formation attacking Lieutenant Wehner, who was above and on one side. I started climbing to join the fight when two EA attacked me from the rear. I turned on them, opening both guns on the leader. We came head on until within a few yards of each other when my opponent turned to one side in a nose dive and I saw him crash to the ground.

'I then turned on the second, shot a short burst, and he turned and went into a dive. I saw a number of EA above but could not find Lieutenant Wehner, so turned and made for our lines. The above fight occurred in the vicinity of St Hilaire. On reaching our balloon line, flew east. Saw Archie on our side, flew toward it, and found an enemy observation machine. I gave chase with some other Spads and got him off from his lines. After a short encounter he crashed within our lines, southeast of Verdun. Lieutenant Wehner is entitled to share in the victories over both the balloons. Confirmations requested, two balloons and three planes.'

As soon as he returned to base, Luke sought Joe Wehner. They had got split up before, but Wehner had always come back. He had become as much a part of Luke as his right arm, the only true friend he had or would ever have, a kind of extension of himself.

But this time Joe Wehner would not be coming back. He had gone down in flames over Labeuville.

Luke was inconsolable. For the rest of that day he spoke to no one, refusing food. That evening he sat alone in his darkened room, brooding. The next morning his commanding officer, recognizing the danger signals, sent him off on a fortnight's leave to Paris. If only Luke could get blind drunk, or find solace with a woman, he might be able to forget the agony a twenty-three-year-old feels, who has just lost his best friend. . . .

It was no use. After only a week Luke was back at the airfield, thirsting for another crack at the enemy. He sought and obtained permission to move up to an old French airfield closer to the front line. His new wingman was Lieutenant Ivan Roberts, and the pair made their first flight together on 26 September. Over Sivry they got mixed up in a fight with five Fokkers; Luke sent one down out of control, but had to break off the fight when his guns jammed. On his return to base he found that Roberts was missing. The lieutenant was never seen again.

It was Joe Wehner all over again, and Luke was plunged into deeper gloom than ever. On 27 September he absented himself from his squadron and was gone until the following morning, when he returned and reported that he had paid a visit to an airfield occupied by the famous French *Escadrille des Cigognes*. He laconically added that he had got another balloon.

His squadron commander administered a severe reprimand, telling Luke that he was grounded until further notice. Luke went out, slamming the door behind him, and a few minutes later – despite his co's order – he took off again, heading for the French airfield near Verdun. The day before, he had pinpointed the position of three more balloons, and he was determined to get them. He knew that when he returned to base, he would probably have to face a court martial; that would probably mean the end of his flying, and he was still burning to avenge Joe Wehner.

He got his three balloons, but he was destined never to face the court – or to wear on his chest the medals for gallantry that had already been awarded to him.

In the muddy field near Murvaux, German soldiers spread out and surrounded him. Their commander called out to him to surrender. Luke's answer was to raise his revolver and snap off several rapid shots towards his enemies. He died almost instantly, hit in the chest by their return fire.

It was only seventeen days since Frank Luke had scored his first official victory, on 12 September, yet in those seventeen days he had destroyed eighteen balloons and aircraft. It was a record that no American airman would ever equal. Ironically, the greatest tribute to his skill and courage was paid by the man who had suffered most at his hands: Lieutenant Mangels, who commanded the balloon company in the Verdun sector. It was Mangels' machine-gunners who shot Luke down, and he was one of the first officers to reach the scene at Murvaux. Mangels ended his report on the incident with these words:

'His insignia I took and kept in remembrance of this great and fearless sportsman. He was a man of dazzling courage, one of the bravest we fought in the war.'

14 Guynemer: the Legend

On 19 July 1915 a young French pilot wrote this terse account of his first victory in his diary. He was flying a Morane Parasol monoplane, and Lieutenant Guerder was his gunner.

'Set off with Guerder after a Boche reported at Courvres and caught up with him over Pierrefonds. Shot one belt, machine-gun jammed, then unjammed. The Boche fled and landed in the direction of Laon. At Coucy we turned back and saw an Aviatik going towards Soissons at about 3200 metres. We followed him, and as soon as he was inside our lines we dived and placed ourselves about fifty metres under and behind him to the left. At our first salvo the Aviatik lurched and we saw part of the machine break. He replied with rifle fire, one bullet hitting a wing and another grazing Guerder's head and hand. At our next shots the pilot slumped down in the cockpit, the observer raised his arms as if in supplication to the sky, and the Aviatik fell straight down in flames between the trenches. . . .'

For Corporal Georges Guynemer, the road to the cockpit of a fighting aeroplane, and the elation of his first success, had been long and hard. As a child, he was too frail and sickly to enjoy much in the way of outdoor sports;

instead, he threw himself wholeheartedly into his studies, specializing in mathematics and Latin. Like his future adversary Max Immelmann he was fascinated by anything mechanical, and the exploits of early aviators such as Louis Bleriot filled him with deep admiration.

Guynemer was the last of a long line of distinguished soldiers, and when the war came in 1914 he was among the first to present himself at a recruiting centre. To his utter dismay, he failed the medical examination. He tried three more times during the next few months, and each time the army doctors refused to pass him. Finally, in desperation, he took matters into his own hands and went to see Captain Bernard-Thierry, an old friend of his father's who commanded the aviation training school at Pau. Bernard-Thierry, greatly impressed by young Guynemer's enthusiasm and technical knowledge, managed to pull the necessary strings – and Georges was accepted as a student mechanic. It was just about the most lowly position in the French Air Corps, but Guynemer was happy for the time being. He soon acquired an intimate technical knowledge of aircraft, and as his confidence in his own ability grew he became more determined to become a pilot.

Once again, his father's influence paid dividends. Many of the young officers with whom Guynemer the elder had begun his military career were now generals, and a quiet word in the ear of one of them resulted in Georges' name being added to a list of successful applicants for flying training. He made his first flight in a Bleriot on 1 February 1915, and went solo five weeks later.

He soon proved to be an exceptional pilot. He nursed his aircraft lovingly, and was completely at one with it; he knew every sound, every vibration it made, just as though his machine was a sentient thing with a personality of its own. Despite his frail body, flying never tired him;

he was completely master of his new element, and excellent eyesight and hearing compensated for his other physical defects.

Early in June 1915, Guynemer – with new corporal's chevrons on his sleeve – was assigned to *Escadrille* MS3 at Vauciennes, where he flew a Morane Parasol two-seater on artillery observation duties. He sometimes took enormous risks to enable his observer to bring back good photographs, which caused his superiors some anxiety. His co, Lieutenant de Beauchamp, told him: 'Be a little more cautious. Take a good look round and size up the situation before you make a move, and when you're in the air never, *never* take unnecessary risks.'

But Guynemer went on taking risks, and on 19 July 1915 he went looking for trouble. He found it, and his first enemy aircraft went down in flames. The exploit earned him the Military Medal, and opened a scoreboard that was only to be closed after he had sent fifty-four machines crashing to destruction.

By the end of the year Guynemer's score had risen to four, placing him at the head of France's growing band of air fighters. Behind him came Jean Navarre, with three victories, and Charles Nungesser and Maxime Lenoir, with two each. Three more 'kills' during the early weeks of 1916 increased the young ace's lead by an even greater margin.

In March 1916 *Escadrille* MS3 was sent to Verdun, where the Germans were throwing all their resources into a desperate bid to smash the French fortress line. Guynemer arrived on the thirteenth, and that same day his promising career almost came to an abrupt end when he had a brush with three Fokker monoplanes over the Argonne. Two bullets struck him in the left arm, while slivers of metal ripped open his cheeks and left eyelid – fortunately without damaging the eye itself. Streaming with blood, he managed to make a forced landing at Brocourt after shaking off his attackers.

For the next few weeks, he fumed impotently in a Paris hospital while other pilots equalled his score – and surpassed it – in the embattled sky over Verdun. By the third week in April he had had enough of antiseptic and doctors; he discharged himself and reported back to his unit on the twenty-sixth, expecting to be greeted like a prodigal son. He was disappointed. His commanding officer took one look at him and immediately sent him back to the rear for a period of convalescence. He did not return for another three weeks.

During the summer of 1917 Guynemer worked hard to perfect his own brand of air fighting tactics. Whereas most other pilots favoured manoeuvring to get into position on an adversary's tail, Guynemer advocated the direct approach from any quarter. Like Albert Ball, he mastered the technique of the frontal attack, maintaining that the vulnerable points of an aircraft were propeller, engine, radiator and pilot, in that order, and that the frontal attack afforded the best chance of hitting one or more of them.

September 1916 was the month in which Guynemer rose to fame like a meteor. On the twenty-third he encountered three Fokkers over the front line and shot down all of them within minutes. His terse combat report reads:

'At 11.20 shot down a Boche in flames near Ache. At 11.21, forced down another Boche out of control near Carrepuy. At 11.25, shot down a Boche in flames near Roye.'

Guynemer's elation at this triple victory was short-lived. Seconds after hitting his third victim, a French 75-mm shell exploded on his starboard pair of wings. The Spad turned upside down and went into a fast spin, dropping through four thousand feet before it eventually recovered. With only partial control, Guynemer crash-landed in the French lines at over a hundred miles an hour, his aircraft breaking up. Guynemer was saved by a special shoulder harness he had fitted to the cockpit; without it he would have been thrown out and probably killed. As it was, he escaped with bruises and a badly cut knee. He was pulled out of the wreck by some excited infantrymen, who carried him off to meet their general. The latter had been just about to review his troops when Guynemer literally dropped in, and now he insisted that the ace join him in taking the salute. Afterwards, the troops took Guynemer to see the charred remains of his victims. On one of the bodies, he found a photograph of an attractive girl. On the back were the words: 'I wish you all the success in the world in your flying. Love, Gretchen.' Guynemer tossed it aside and it fluttered away. He felt no emotion. He had won, the other had lost. That was all.

Later, in the mess, Guynemer's comrades laughingly pinned up a recipe for 'boiled egg à la Guynemer'. It read: 'Take an egg. Put it in boiling water when Guynemer goes into action. Wait until he has shot down three aircraft, then remove and eat.'

This triple success brought Guynemer's score to eighteen. Close behind came Nungesser with seventeen, while Navarre was in third place with twelve. By the end of the year Guynemer's score had risen to twenty-five; he celebrated his twenty-second birthday, on 26 December, by shooting down two enemy aircraft. One of them, an Albatros, he disposed of after firing just fifteen rounds, killing the enemy pilot with a burst of fire in the kidneys.

In the spring of 1917 Guynemer's unit – now universally known as the '*Escadrille des Cigognes*' – was transferred from the Somme to Lorraine, where its pilots were responsible for the air defence of the Nancy sector. Day after day, the inhabitants of Nancy and the surrounding villages were treated to a grandstand spectacle as French and German aircraft twisted in savage dogfights over their heads.

On 16 March Guynemer, together with Lieutenants Deullin and Dorme, was patrolling over Auger, the three pilots quartering a narrow sector of sky – a rough square whose sides measured three miles by three. Within that square, in the space of twelve minutes, the three shot down four enemy aircraft. Guynemer destroyed two of them, and completed his hat-trick by shooting down an Albatros in the same sector that afternoon.

His score mounted steadily during the murderous summer of 1917, the months that marked the deadliest struggle for air supremacy over the western front. He was now the most decorated of all French pilots, but even when he was on leave he seldom wore his medals, preferring to keep them tucked carelessly away in a tunic pocket. It seemed he bore a charmed life; he had been forced down no fewer than eight times during air fights, and each time he had escaped with only minor injuries. He made light of the continual risks he ran. 'People can no longer say that I am a weakling,' he wrote to his sisters. 'I flick bullets away from me with my finger-tips.'

Although his colleagues were always advising him to be more cautious, he continually pressed home his attacks against superior odds, ignoring the fire directed at him. Privately, however, he knew that his luck could not last. To his friend and fellow-pilot Jean Constantin, he confided: 'I have got away with it for too long. I have a feeling that one of these days I am not going to come back.'

As the summer wore on, Guynemer seemed gripped by a morbid fatalism. On more than one occasion, he mentioned to his friends that he would meet his end soon

after he had destroyed his fiftieth enemy. That happened
in August 1917, and on the twenty-eighth of that month,
during a spell of leave in Paris, he told an old school friend:
'I'll be back in action soon, but you won't see my name
in the *communiqués* any more. It's all over. I've got my fiftieth Boche': and later, to a priest who was an old family
friend, he said flatly: 'I'm as good as finished. I won't get
away next time.'

Guynemer's father noted that Georges appeared tired
and listless; his former enthusiasm seemed to have burned
away. The elder Guynemer advised his son to have a rest.
He could still carry on flying, training other pilots for a
time before returning to his unit. 'There's a limit to what
a human being can take,' he pointed out.

'Yes,' replied Georges, 'there's a limit all right, and one
has to keep on striving to pass it. I feel that unless you have
given everything there is to give, and a little more besides,
you have really given nothing at all.'

It appears that in the summer of 1917 Guynemer was
showing all the symptoms of what would nowadays be
diagnosed as combat fatigue. When he returned to his unit
in September, his comrades noted how his face had
changed. It became satanic, almost terrible to look upon,
whenever he climbed into the cockpit of his aircraft. It was
in many ways like the face of a drug addict: but the drug,
in Guynemer's case, was combat.

On the morning of 11 September 1917 Guynemer
seemed particularly nervous, pacing up and down anxiously while his mechanics prepared his aircraft for flight.
He was scheduled to fly a patrol with three other pilots,
but two were a little late in arriving and Guynemer im-
patiently decided to take off with only one companion,
Lieutenant Bozon-Verduraz.

A couple of hours later, Bozon-Verduraz returned –
alone. There had been a dogfight, and he had lost

sight of Guynemer. His combat report tells the terse story:

'Pilot: Bozon-Verduraz. Take-off time: 8.35. Time of landing: 10.25. Maximum altitude: 5,900.

'At 9.25, together with Captain Guynemer, attacked an enemy two-seater over the lines at Poelcapelle. Made one pass and fired thirty rounds. Captain Guynemer continued to pursue the enemy as I was obliged to break off to avoid eight single-seaters, which were preparing to attack me. I did not see Captain Guynemer again. At 10.20, attacked a two-seater at 5900 over Poperinghe. Fired ten rounds at point-blank range, then gun jammed. Pursued the enemy, but was unable to clear the stoppage and returned to base.'

The hours ticked by. Guynemer was long overdue. Commandant Brocard, co of the *Cigognes*, spent all morning on the telephone, searching for news; there was none. Then, in the afternoon, there came a message from an infantry unit to say that a French aircraft had been seen diving into the German lines. There was nothing to say that this had been Guynemer, and his fellow pilots continued to pray for a miracle. Perhaps he had been forced down and taken prisoner....

Then, three days later, the hopes were shattered. It was a German newspaper that carried the grim tidings: 'Captain Wissemann has shot down the French ace Guynemer.'

It was another month before the news was officially confirmed. In response to a note sent via the Spanish Embassy, the Department of Foreign Affairs in Berlin issued the following statement:

'Captain Guynemer fell in the course of an air fight at 10 am on 11 September last, close to Cemetery of Honour No. II to the south of Poelcapelle. A medical examination revealed that the index finger of the left hand had been shot away, and that the cause of death was a bullet in the head.'

Some time later on that September morning, the British artillery had laid down a heavy barrage over the area where Guynemer was said to have fallen. A German patrol which combed the smoking, shell-cratered ground in its wake found no trace of either Guynemer or his aircraft.

At the time of his death, Guynemer had logged 666 flying hours and had destroyed fifty-three enemy aircraft, earning twenty-six citations. On one occasion he had shot down four aircraft in a single sortie, and his other victories included one hat-trick and six doubles. He was just twenty-two years old.

His body was never found, a fact that added to the considerable legend that already surrounded him. Schoolchildren said of him: 'He flew so high, on and on in the sky, that he could never come to earth again.'

It was a fitting epitaph for one of the greatest pilots of all time.

15 René Fonck: Ace of Aces

A week or so after the death of Georges Guynemer, Captain Wissemann, who claimed to have shot him down, wrote home to his family: 'Don't worry about me. Never again will I meet an adversary who is half as dangerous as Guynemer.'

Only nineteen days after writing those words, Wissemann was shot down and killed by a French Spad fighter. It was flown by a man who was destined to emerge from the holocaust of the First World War as the top-scoring Allied fighter pilot: René Fonck.

In many ways, Fonck was the exact opposite in temperament to the impetuous Guynemer. Although one of the youngest French pilots, he was also one of the most mature. Air fighting for him was a matter of science, and he became a master of tact and cunning. He spent long hours studying his opponents' air fighting tactics, and as his experience grew he came up with an answer to all of them.

Joining the French Air Corps in the spring of 1915, Fonck spent the first two years of his flying career as a reconnaissance pilot, and it was in this role that he had his first encounters with the enemy. His very first combat report, dated 2 July 1915, was very brief: 'While carrying out a reconnaissance in the Münster area I came upon a German aircraft and fired several rounds at it with my carbine. It escaped.'

Seventy-five other German airmen who tangled with Fonck before the armistice in 1918 were to be far less fortunate. Nevertheless, he had his fair share of narrow escapes, mostly during his time as an observation pilot. On one occasion he took off on a reconnaissance and artillery spotting mission in the Verdun sector in May 1916, together with another pilot named Sergeant Noel. The two aircraft were patrolling over Loges Wood, not far from Roye, when a terrific anti-aircraft barrage suddenly erupted all around them. As he fought to control his own aircraft on the violent shock waves, Fonck saw Noel's machine take a direct hit only a few feet away. Horrified, he watched the wings tear away and the debris of the fuselage plummet earthwards, trailing a banner of smoke.

'Fascinated and sickened by the catastrophe,' Fonck wrote later, 'I strayed into the slipstream of Noel's plunging aircraft and spun down myself, recovering only a few hundred feet from the ground. The German gunners must have thought they had accounted for both of us at the same time.'

It was over the fearful battleground of the Somme, in the summer of 1916, that Fonck scored his early series of victories. Violent air combats were a daily occurrence over the Somme, with formations of Fokkers up to twenty strong crossing the front line like shoals of silver fish and pouncing on the Allied reconnaissance aircraft, which normally flew in twos and threes. Air armament was still in the enemy's favour; despite the introduction of the new British Lewis guns, with their 100-cartridge ammunition drums, the Germans retained a definite superiority with their machine-guns firing forwards through the propeller arc. On the other hand, the French Nieuport Scout, with which many front-line squadrons were then re-equipping, was a superlative and highly manœuvrable fighter, and the Germans no longer had things all their own way. Allied combat experience was building up all the time, and an experienced pilot could give a splendid account of himself even when flying a slow reconnaissance aircraft such as the Caudron G4.

Such was the case with René Fonck, who, on 6 August 1916, was on a photographic mission over Roye with Lieutenant Thiberge as his observer. He was attacked by two Fokkers but managed to outmanœuvre both of them, and encouraged by this success he went looking for trouble. Some distance away, a series of white 75-mm shell bursts seemed to indicate the presence of more enemy aircraft, and he headed towards them. At last he spotted them: two Rumplers, circling over Noyon. One of them made off immediately, but Fonck cut off the other's avenue of escape. For twenty minutes the two aircraft circled one another as the German tried desperately to get away.

'I kept right on top of him,' the French pilot said later. 'I countered every one of his manœuvres, opposing turn for turn, dive for dive. After a while, his machine-gunner ceased firing at us and simply stared, white-faced, as though hypnotized.' The German eventually gave up and went down to land behind the French lines. He and his observer were taken prisoner. Later, under interrogation, the German pilot admitted: 'I couldn't do a thing. My adversary had me under his control all the time. He blocked every manœuvre I made, dominating me all the time. He had me completely at his mercy.' It was the only time that the crew would escape unharmed from a German aircraft that fell victim to Fonck's expertise.

Fonck was still flying Caudrons in the spring of 1917, when some of the bloodiest air fighting of the war took place. On 17 March that year, Fonck had what he later described as the stiffest air fight of his whole career. With

Lieutenant Marcaggi as his observer, he had taken off that morning to carry out a reconnaissance mission together with another Caudron, flown by Sergeant Raux. Some ten miles inside the enemy lines, Fonck spotted five Albatros scouts flying in perfect v formation. Although for the two Caudrons to engage the speedy German fighters was rather like a pair of ducks attacking hawks, Fonck signalled to Raux that he intended to go into action. Raux acknowledged and the Caudrons dived towards the enemy, the wind howling in their bracing wires.

For several minutes the seven aircraft twisted wildly, their machine-guns hammering, until inevitably the Albatros – with their higher speed and greater manœuvrability – gained the upper hand. Three of them trapped Raux's aircraft and within seconds it was hurtling earthwards, a blazing torch. The pilot managed to recover and make a forced landing in the French lines. Terribly burned about the face and hands, he clawed his way out of the burning debris – a funeral pyre that contained the bullet-torn body of his observer – before collapsing.

For once in his life, Fonck threw caution to the winds when he saw Raux's machine go down. Throwing himself at the three aircraft that had shot down his colleague, he opened fire on one of them at close range and the Albatros fell apart. The others broke in all directions and dived away over their own territory. Nevertheless, Fonck was forced to acknowledge that it had been a close call.

Shortly after this fight, Fonck's application to join a single-seat scout unit – which had been lodged for some time – was approved, and on 25 April 1917, to his utter delight, he was posted to the famous *Escadrille des Cigognes*, which was then based at Bonne-Maison airfield near Nîmes. His first interview with the co, Commandant Brocard, was brief in the extreme; in fact, it was all over in three sentences.

'What we do here,' said Brocard, 'is shoot down as many Boches as possible.'

'I'll do my best,' was Fonck's reply.

'I know that,' grinned Brocard, and dismissed the young pilot with a wave of his hand. So it was that René Fonck achieved a long-standing desire, and found himself attached to *Escadrille* 103 under the command of a celebrated fighter pilot, Captain d'Harcourt. It was to be only a matter of days before the newcomer proved his worth; on 3 May he caught two enemy two-seaters, artillery spotting over the front lines, and shot down one of them near Berry-au-Bac.

Fonck arrived at a time when the sands were running out for some of the veterans of the *Cigognes*. One of the first to go was René Dorme, who had been with the *escadrille* since early 1916 and had shot down twenty enemy aircraft. Known affectionately as 'father', he was, at twenty-two, older than most of his colleagues. He was shot down and killed at the end of May 1917, and Fonck, who had become a close friend, set out to avenge him. His chance came on 12 June, when he outfought Captain von Baer – the commander of one of Germany's top fighter squadrons, with a personal score of twelve – and sent him down in flames.

In July 1917 the *Cigognes* left the Lorraine sector for a new airfield near Dunkirk. The Germans bade them farewell by bombing their old airfield on the night of their departure, but no one was seriously hurt. The new move was part of an overall plan that called for the concentration of the French fighter *escadrilles* in Flanders, where – together with the RFC – they were to establish air superiority in support of a major Allied offensive that was soon to begin. Here, for the first time, large-scale ground attack operations were carried out by the fighter units, with devastating effect on the closely packed enemy troops and supply columns. The terrain, however, was by no means in the favour of any pilot who had to make a forced landing. 'In front of us,' wrote Fonck, 'there was nothing but miles and miles of spongy ground, where water crept stealthily into the tiniest hole. The whole area was a vast quagmire that could swallow up an object as big as a tank without trace.'

Gone, now, were the days of what the French called '*la chasse libre*', where pilots hunted the enemy in ones and twos. By the autumn of 1917, teamwork had become the order of the day, and there was no finer team anywhere than the *Cigognes*.

After avenging the death of Guynemer in September 1917, there seemed to be no holding René Fonck. October was his month; during it, he destroyed ten enemy aircraft in the course of thirteen and a half hours' flying time. His tactics were simple enough. He would fly high, so that he was almost always above his opponents; then, choosing his moment carefully, he would use his height and speed advantage to gain surprise. His aim was excellent, and a single firing pass on the dive was usually enough to send an enemy down in flames.

By the end of the year, his personal score stood at nineteen enemy aircraft destroyed, putting him in equal third place with two more talented pilots, Deullin and Madon. In second place was Captain Heurtaux, with twenty-one, and top of the list came Charles Nungesser, with thirty. He was the senior surviving French pilot, in terms of 'kills'.

The *Cigognes* returned to the Verdun sector in January 1918, and Fonck soon made his presence felt. On the nineteenth, while patrolling with Captain d'Harcourt and another pilot named Fontaine, he encountered a superior formation of enemy aircraft over the front. In the middle of the ensuing fight, Fonck noticed that Fontaine was in difficulty, his engine having apparently failed, and was being harassed by two German machines. Fonck quickly shot down his own adversary, then dived on Fontaine's attackers. Within seconds one of them, too, was spinning down in flames. The other fled and Fontaine made a safe emergency landing.

Fonck's personal score grew steadily during the early weeks of 1918. One of his victims was a German two-seater whose unnamed pilot had become notorious because of his highly accurate trench-strafing attacks; the French pilots called him 'Fantomas' and several claimed to have shot him down during November and December 1917, but he always turned up again. Then Fonck caught him one February morning and scattered his burning debris over the frozen earth of no-man's land.

Soon afterwards, in March 1918, came the last great German push of the war: the Ludendorff Offensive, with masses of men and material rolling forward on a broad front from the Swiss frontier to Belgium. From Verdun the *Cigognes* were switched to Champagne, where some of the heaviest fighting took place. Day after day the fighter squadrons flew low over the front, endlessly strafing the enemy columns and inflicting terrible casualties. 'All day long,' wrote Fonck, 'the air was filled with the roar of engines. We flew so low that we almost touched the enemy's bayonets, watching the compact masses of troops wilt away before our machine-gun fire. The chaos was terrible. Panic-stricken horses charged in all directions, trampling soldiers underfoot.'

The slaughter brought about a profound change in many of the young pilots, including Fonck. Hitherto, the war for them had been an impersonal affair; a burst of gun-fire, a flash of flame streaking back from an enemy aircraft, a ribbon of smoke that marked its end. Somehow, the man in the cockpit seemed unreal. Now, for the first time, they saw the deadly effect of their bullets on human flesh from a range of only yards, and were sickened by it. The war, after March 1918, became something to be ended as quickly as possible; that was the new determination in the hearts of boys who had suddenly become men.

It was air power, more than any other single factor, that halted the great German offensive and gave the reeling Allied armies time to consolidate. As the front lines stabilized again, massive artillery exchanges became the order of the day, and the activities of observation aircraft on both sides assumed new importance. The fighter pilots once again had a field day, but now it was the Allies who were masters of the sky. By the third week in April Fonck's score had risen to thirty-six enemy aircraft destroyed; he and his aircraft seemed to be welded together to form a single deadly killing machine. He was meticulous in his approach to air fighting, constantly devising new methods of exercising his vision, heart, muscles and reflexes as well as making sure that his machine and its armament were technically perfect. To cut down the risk of his guns jamming – which had been responsible for the death of many a pilot at a crucial moment in a dogfight – he invented a simple device for checking the calibre of every bullet in his ammunition belts. If there was the slightest sign of imperfection, the bullet was eliminated.

He brought his own brand of science to air combat, spending hours of his precious leisure time working out such things as relative speeds and deflection angles. He inspected as many shot-down enemy aircraft as possible, not because of any macabre fascination, as was the case with Guynemer, but because he wanted to work out the 'dead spots' in the enemy's field of vision. In the air, Fonck's economy in the use of ammunition was almost legendary; he seldom used more than a dozen bullets to despatch an adversary. Correct positioning and superb marksmanship were Fonck's twin secrets; he could hit a one-franc piece with a rifle bullet when most other people could not even see the coin.

He attributed much of his success to the five hundred hours he had spent flying two-seater reconnaissance machines. 'You have to be careful when you are attacking a two-seater,' he said, 'and remember that it is armed at both front and rear. Having flown this type of machine for so long, I knew exactly what it could do, and how it could always be shot down by a more manœuvrable single-seater flown by a pilot who knew what he was doing.'

Fonck was the first real specimen of a new breed of fighter pilot; a cold, calculating scientist for whom amateurism had no place in combat. He worked out every move in the minutest detail, leaving nothing to chance. He knew that lack of attention to detail killed far more pilots than the enemy; he had seen many of his friends die because they had not taken sufficient care of their machine-gun, or their engine, or because they had drunk too much brandy the night before. Methodically, he set about reducing the part played by the traditional 'pilot's luck' in his personal survival to the barest minimum.

Nevertheless, he was by no means inhuman. He gave his novice pilots every possible encouragement, even crediting his own 'kills' to them. He was never 'kill-conscious', like many of his fellow pilots; what mattered to Fonck was the ability to survive, and shooting down Germans came very much in second place.

Despite this attitude – or perhaps because of it – shooting down Germans seemed to come to him with astonishing ease. On 9 May 1918, for example, he shot down no fewer than six aircraft in a single day, the first three all within the space of a minute. He landed to refuel and have something to eat; then, at 6.40 pm, he destroyed a fourth aircraft, followed by another at 6.45 and a sixth ten seconds later. The destruction of all six had cost him just fifty-two rounds of ammunition.

By the middle of July 1918 the twenty-four-year-old Fonck had been officially credited with the destruction of forty-nine enemy aircraft. He was now ten ahead of Charles Nungesser, who had only just returned to combat after several weeks in hospital following a bad crash. On 15 July the *Cigognes* were ordered to a new base in the Champagne sector, where the Germans had unleashed a severe attack on the river Marne. As soon as he arrived, Fonck decided to make a first-hand survey of the combat zone before landing and quickly discovered that a number of German pilots seemed to have had the same notion. There were enemy aircraft everywhere, all apparently oblivious of the presence of the lone Frenchman, and he singled out one formation that looked particularly interesting; it consisted of a pair of two-seaters escorted by half a dozen Fokker DVIIs. Despite the fact that his cockpit was encumbered by two suitcases, not to mention a dozen bottles of wine, Fonck nosed over into a screaming dive, ripped through the startled Fokkers and, in a single murderous pass, sent both two-seaters down in flames. Then he headed for home at full throttle, landed, and calmly set about unpacking his things.

The tempo of air fighting was maintained throughout the summer, as the Allied armies broke the last desperate German efforts to achieve supremacy and gradually went over to the offensive all along the front. In August Fonck shot down eleven aircraft in ten days. The pilot of one of them, Lieutenant Wusthoff – himself an ace with twenty-seven victories – lived, and Fonck visited him in hospital. The German confessed that his fellow pilots knew very little about Fonck or his tactics.

'That's not surprising,' the Frenchman told him. 'My opponents don't usually survive to talk about me.'

A few days later, Fonck shot down three German fighters within seconds of each other. All three fell burning in a field, separated by less than a hundred yards. By the end of August, his score had risen to sixty. During September bad weather brought a temporary halt to flying on both sides; then, on the twenty-sixth, the weather cleared and the fighters were unleashed in support of a big Allied counter-offensive on the Marne. Fonck shot down three aircraft that morning, followed by three more in the afternoon. He attacked two more, then his machine-gun jammed and he was forced to return to base.

In the closing weeks of the war he claimed nine more victims, bringing his official score to seventy-five – more than any other Allied pilot. In all his air battles he had never once been wounded, nor had his aircraft suffered serious damage.

After the war Fonck took up a career in civil aviation. In the spring of 1920, while attending a banquet in Stockholm to mark the occasion of the founding of a Swedish airline, he had a curious experience. One evening after dinner, there was a telephone call for him from a young German pilot who had been the last commander of the *Richthofen Geschwader*: Hermann Goering. He had left the chaos of post-war Germany and for some time had been eking out a living by giving pleasure flights; now, desperately anxious to get a job in commercial aviation, he asked Fonck to put in a good word for him. Fonck, anxious to help a pilot and former adversary, never hesitated. He dropped a word in the right quarter, and Goering got a job with the new airline.

Years later, this incident was to have unforeseen repercussions. Following the Franco-German armistice of June 1940, Fonck was summoned to Vichy by Marshal Philippe Pétain, who asked the pilot if he would visit Goering, exploit his old contact, and try and sound out Hitler's intentions with regard to Vichy France.

As Pétain's emissary, Fonck visited Goering several times during the next two years, and the two became friendly. In 1945, however, when the leaders of Vichy France were placed on trial, some of the mud thrown at them inevitably lodged on Fonck. Almost overnight, he fell from his status as a national hero to something approaching a criminal; old friends avoided him, forgetting his former exploits – just as France conveniently forgot that Pétain himself had been the 'Hero of Verdun' in the former war.

So, after thirty years, the star that had risen to its ascendancy over the bloody earth of the First World War waned at last, eclipsed by spite and bitterness in a world that knew nothing of the howl of the wind in the wires, or the taut drumming of fabric on an aircraft's wing.

Glossary of Aircraft Types mentioned in the text

AEG: reconnaissance biplanes produced by the Germans in 1915–16. Most widely used type was the AEG CIV, armed with two machine-guns. It could carry up to 90 kg of bombs in the rear cockpit and had a maximum speed of 98 mph.

Albatros: series of biplane fighters in service with the German Flying Corps. The Albatros DI, which entered service in August 1916, was the first fighter to carry an efficient two-gun armament, and equipped the first German *Jagdstaffeln*. The Albatros DIII, which appeared in January 1917, was the best known of the Albatros types and saw a great deal of action against the Allies in 'Bloody April' of that year.

BE2: observation biplane produced by the Royal Aircraft Factory, 1912–14. The BE equipped the first RFC squadrons to go to France in 1914. These machines suffered very heavily at the hands of the early Fokkers in 1915.

Bristol F2B 'Fighter': two-seat fighter biplane which entered service with the RFC in March 1917. Served with seven RFC squadrons on the Western Front and was one of the most successful British fighters of World War I.

Caudron: series of French two-seat bomber and reconnaissance aircraft. The Caudron GIII served with Allied air forces, 1914–18, and was also widely used for training; the GIV was a twin-engined machine which could carry a 220-lb bomb load. GIVs were used by the British Royal Naval Air Service to attack Zeppelin sheds in Belgium.

DFW: German two-seat reconnaissance and training aircraft used during 1914–15. Well liked for its pleasant flying characteristics.

Farman: French designs originating in 1913, the Farman MF7 'Longhorn' and MF11 'Shorthorn' served widely as bombing, observation and training aircraft with all Allied air forces. One

MF11 serving with the RNAS made the first night bombing raid of the war.

FE2b: two-seat scout biplanes designed by the Royal Aircraft Factory in 1915. Powered by a 'pusher' engine, the 'Fee' was armed with two machine-guns and saw much action with the RFC during the air battles of 1916. Also used in limited numbers for night bombing.

Fokker DI–DV: series of single-seat biplane scouts which entered service with the German Flying Corps from mid-1916. The early Fokker D Types were generally inferior to other German fighters then entering service and did not have a distinguished career.

Fokker DVII: single-seat biplane scout which entered service with von Richthofen's *Jagdgeschwader* I in April 1918 and which served widely until the end of the war. Acclaimed as the best German fighter of World War I.

Fokker DrI: fighter triplane which entered service with von Richthoften's *Jagdgeschwader* I in August 1917. The 'Red Baron' was shot down and killed while flying one of these machines, as was Werner Voss. Widely used during the spring of 1918 before being replaced by the DVII.

Fokker E Types: the Fokker 'E' Type monoplanes, fitted with a synchronized machine-gun firing through the propeller arc, gave the Germans almost complete air superiority over the Western Front in the autumn and winter of 1915. Max Immelmann scored most of his victories while flying these machines.

Friedrichshafen G Types: series of twin-engined bombers which served with the German Flying Corps. Used mainly to attack targets in France and Belgium. The GIII, used in 1917–18, could carry 500 kg of bombs.

Gotha GI–GV: twin-engined German bombers, widely used during 1916–18. The GIVs carried out several raids on the south of England in the summer of 1917, and these were continued at night by the more powerful GV early in 1918. The Gothas were well armed with three machine-guns and proved very difficult to shoot down.

Halberstadt CL Types: two-seat escort and ground attack biplanes which entered service with the German Flying Corps early in 1917. Armed with three machine-guns, they could carry a load of small bombs or hand grenades. They played a major part against Allied ground forces in the battle of Cambrai, November 1917.

LFG (Roland) CII: two-seat observation aircraft widely used by the Germans in 1916. Captain Albert Ball, VC, shot down one of these machines to score his first victory.

LVG 'C' Types: armed reconnaissance two-seaters used extensively by the Germans from 1915 to the end of the war. One CII made a daring daylight raid on London in November 1916, dropping six bombs on Victoria station.

Fighter Pilots of World War I

Morane Type L: known as the MS3 in military service, the Morane was a single-seat biplane fighter used widely by the French and also by the RNAS. The French ace Georges Guynemer was flying one of these machines when he scored his fist victory.

Nieuport 11–17: series of single-seat biplane fighters used extensively by all the Allied air arms. The Nieuport 11, nicknamed 'Baby', helped to overcome the Fokker menace in 1916. The Nieuport 11 and 16 equipped most leading French units as well as squadrons of the RFC and RNAS, and a more powerful development, the Nieuport 17, became one of the most successful of all Allied fighters. Equipped with Le Prieur rockets, it was used widely for balloon busting.

Pfalz DIII: widely-used German fighter biplane which equipped 46 *Jagdstaffeln* during 1917–18. It was an excellent gun platform and could absorb a lot of battle damage, but German pilots generally preferred the faster Albatros.

SE5: single-seat biplane fighter which entered service with the RFC (No. 56 Squadron) in March 1917. The type did much to help re-establish Allied air superiority and was flown by most of the RFC's leading aces.

Sopwith Camel: single-seat biplane fighter which reached the front-line squadrons of the RFC in the summer of 1917. A difficult type to fly, it nevertheless destroyed more enemy aircraft than any other Allied type and could out-turn most enemy fighters. Over 2,500 Camels were in service with the RFC at the end of World War I.

Sopwith Snipe: single-seat biplane fighter designed to replace the Camel. Entered service with the RAF in the summer of 1918, and continued to serve with many RAF squadrons after the end of the war.

Sopwith Triplane: highly manœuvrable scout which served with RNAS squadrons on the Western Front in 1917. Was very successful and made such an impact among the enemy that no fewer than fourteen German and Austrian aircraft manufacturers were asked to submit new designs as an 'answer' to it. It had still not been outclassed when it began to be replaced by the Camel.

Spad VII and XIII: single-seat biplane fighters which equipped many squadrons of the French *Aviation Militaire*, RFC, RNAS, American Air Service, Italian Air Force and Belgian Air Service. America's leading air ace, Eddie Rickenbacker, flew a Spad, and it was while flying a Spad XIII that Georges Guynemer met his death.